Plymouth's Hidden Railways

Plymouth's Hidden Railways

by

Paul Burkhalter

TWELVEHEADS PRESS

Truro 2017

Front cover main picture

Victoria Wharves' FH 1834 shunting, with mixed gauge track for railway and crane use. 28 June 1961. VICTORIA WHARVES LTD

Front cover bottom left to right

Ernesettle's HE3133 in preservation at Bodmin. 13 May 1990. ROGER HATELEY

WB3121 fireless locomotive at ECC Marsh Mills. 30 May 1971. GORDON EDGAR

Devonport No.2 in North Yard. 1960s. PAUL BURKHALTER COLLECTION

Front cover flap

HC D1363 of 1965 at Esso Bitumen Cattedown. 13 April 2002. ROGER HATELEY INDUSTRIAL RAILWAY SOCIETY

Back cover main picture

RNAD Ernesettle Hunslet 6646 of 1967 was the last operational locomotive, seen here on the Jetty at the end of the narrow gauge use in 1980. PAUL BURKHALTER COLLECTION

Back cover bottom left to right

Victoria Wharves with Planet 3281 in front of the headshunt tunnel. 21 June 1983. ROBIN WAYWELL

Devonport Dockyard newly re-painted Clayton loco's. October 2008. COURTESY BABCOCK MARINE

Devonport Dockyard. One of the ex-Army Drewry's by the Rail Gate to the Barracks. 10 June 2004. PAUL BURKHALTER

Back cover flap

TH125V at Plymstock Cement Works. 21 June 1983. ROBIN WAYWELL

All photographs by Paul Burkhalter or from his collection unless otherwise credited. The author and publisher have made every effort to establish the provenance of photographs and apologise if any copyright has been inadvertently breached

TWELVEHEADS PRESS

First published 2017 by Twelveheads Press

ISBN 978 0 906294 92 5

British Library Cataloguing-in-Publication Data.

A catalogue record for this book is available from the British Library.

Typeset in Garamond

Printed by Short Run Press Ltd, Exeter

Contents

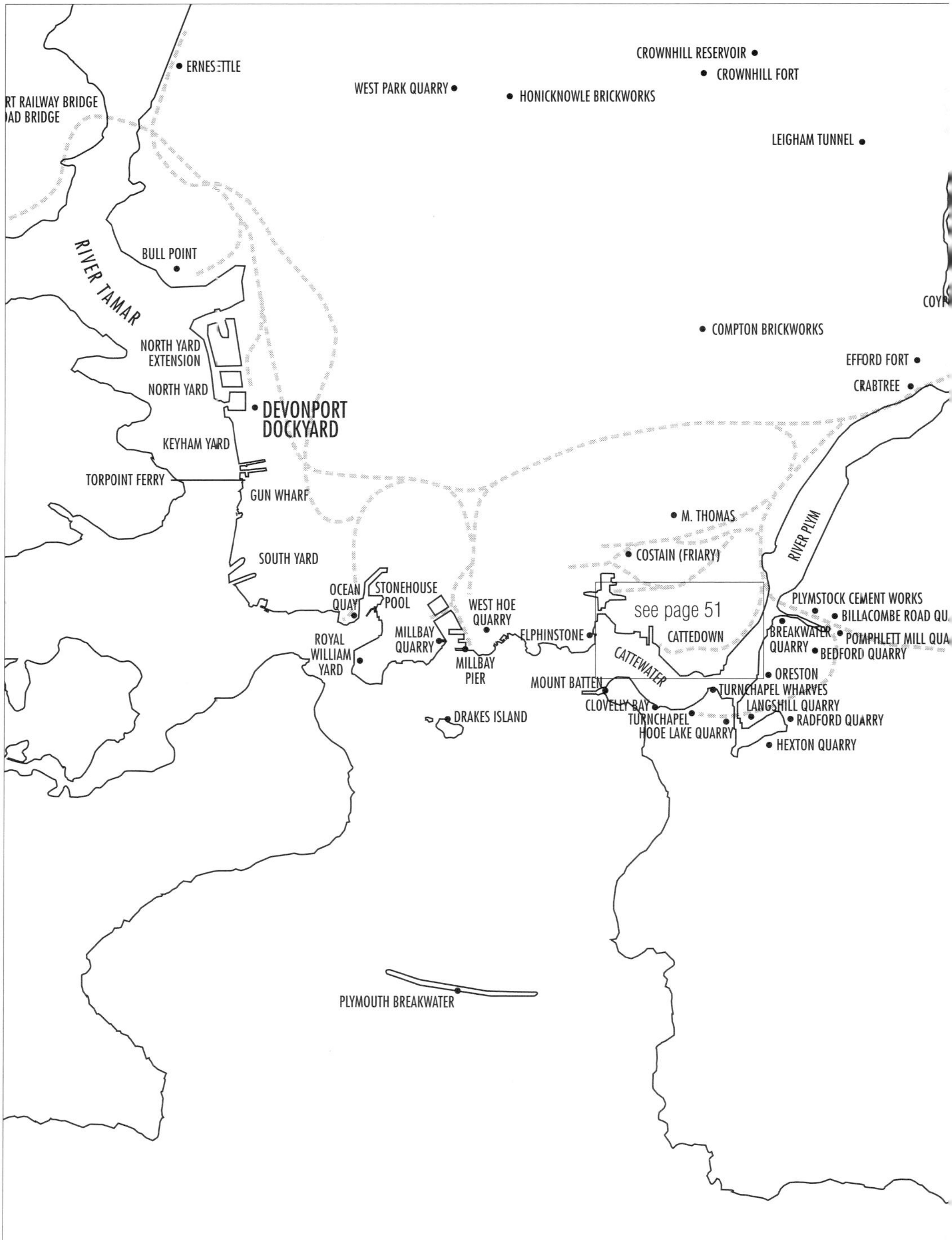

ERNESETTLE
RT RAILWAY BRIDGE
AD BRIDGE
WEST PARK QUARRY
HONICKNOWLE BRICKWORKS
CROWNHILL RESERVOIR
CROWNHILL FORT
LEIGHAM TUNNEL
RIVER TAMAR
BULL POINT
NORTH YARD EXTENSION
NORTH YARD
DEVONPORT DOCKYARD
KEYHAM YARD
TORPOINT FERRY
GUN WHARF
SOUTH YARD
COMPTON BRICKWORKS
EFFORD FORT
CRABTREE
M. THOMAS
COSTAIN (FRIARY)
RIVER PLYM
OCEAN QUAY
STONEHOUSE POOL
WEST HOE QUARRY
ROYAL WILLIAM YARD
MILLBAY QUARRY
MILLBAY PIER
ELPHINSTONE
see page 51
CATTEDOWN
CATTEWATER
PLYMSTOCK CEMENT WORKS
BILLACOMBE ROAD QU
BREAKWATER QUARRY
POMPHLETT MILL QUA
BEDFORD QUARRY
ORESTON
MOUNT BATTEN
CLOVELLY BAY
TURNCHAPEL
TURNCHAPEL WHARVES
LANGSHILL QUARRY
RADFORD QUARRY
HOOE LAKE QUARRY
HEXTON QUARRY
DRAKES ISLAND
PLYMOUTH BREAKWATER

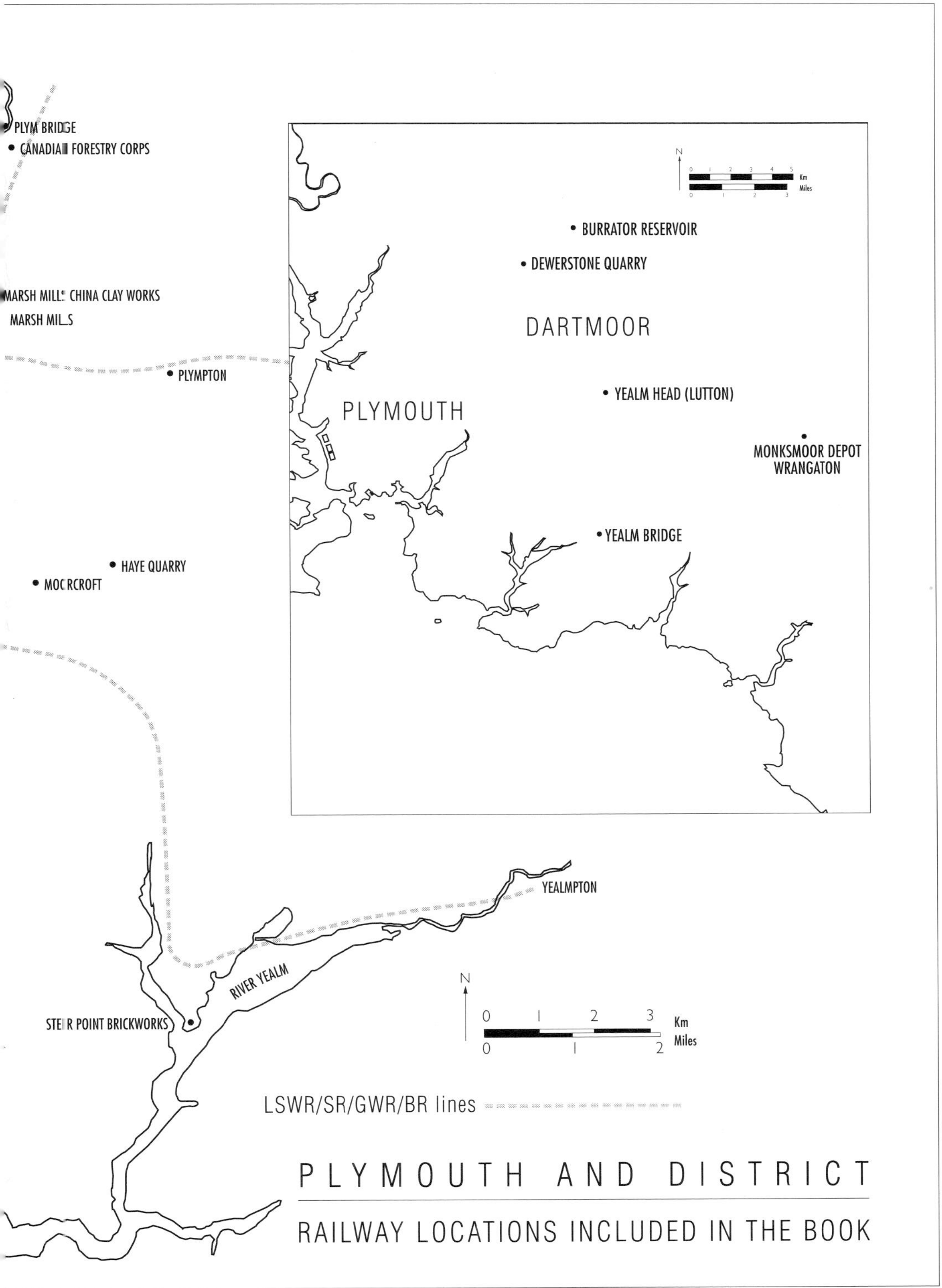

PLYMOUTH AND DISTRICT

RAILWAY LOCATIONS INCLUDED IN THE BOOK

Narrow gauge tracks still in position in RNAD Bullpoint, 36 years after the cessation of traffic. November 1994.
PAUL BURKHALTER

Introduction and acknowledgements

Plymouth is a maritime place. The sea and river predominates life here, either for business or leisure. The Royal Navy was here in the 17th century, and the products of the hinterland were sent out by ship from here. The Dockyard is the largest private employer in the south west peninsula and still dominates the city's life. Even china clay from pits around Dartmoor still departs by sea. It is no surprise that railways were built to serve this sea trade. The earliest were in the 18th century in the Dockyard and at the quarry winning stone for Eddystone Lighthouse. Then in 1818 a public railway from Princetown was proposed, at a similar time to the more well-known Stockton & Darlington Railway.

A 'proper' main-line railway to connect with the rest of the country arrived in 1848, and changed the way of life for many. It was not too long before businesses and the Navy utilised the improved communication this provided. So it continued for a century and more, until the run-down of the small load rail freight service from the 1970s onwards. However, surprisingly, three rail-served sites remain in 2017; Cattewater scrap yard (mothballed), Ernesettle Armaments Depot (very occasionally) and Devonport Dockyard.

The geographical boundaries covered by this book are arbitrary. Obviously the sea and the River Tamar (or Hamoaze as the lower section of the River Tamar is known) form the south and west limits. To the east and north is more random, and I have ventured into the South Hams and the lower slopes of Dartmoor with little reason. To qualify for inclusion here, is that the siding, line, or system was not in the ownership of the main-line companies, viz: Great Western Railway (GWR) and London & South Western Railway (L&SWR), eventually becoming part of British Railways (BR).

AUTHORS NOTE

I started this research in 1993, when setting out to find out about the history of the railway in Devonport Dockyard. I thought there would be a small history on the subject (an Oakwood Press perhaps), instead I ended up writing it myself. Twelveheads Press took on the project and the result appeared in 1996. It went through a second printing in 2002, and has finally gone out of print.

For that project I found myself in a field of railway history I previously knew nothing about – industrial railways – and I quickly found the

Industrial Locomotive Society (ILS) and the Industrial Railway Society (IRS). In 1993 J. B. Latham of the ILS asked me if I would see if the local Plymouth & West Devon Record Office had anything about the Devonport Corporation Crownhill Reservoir, which I researched and answered. This led me to find that this repository had a myriad of fascinating documents, and hence the regular visits to them over the intervening 23 years. The Crownhill material formed the basis of my first article in the *Industrial Locomotive* issue 76 in 1995, my first published industrial railway item. This book is a result of the intervening years of collecting material about the hidden railways of Plymouth. This aspiration to bring fresh information to the public domain depends entirely upon the availability of source material. The varied size of each entry reflects that situation, as most locations were private companies where archiving of material is rarely an activity. A laudable exception is Victoria Wharves who still hold documents from the late 19th century despite the changes in ownership.

However this is the first time all such has been gathered in one place. So that it is all-inclusive, I have included a shortened history of the Devonport Dockyard Railway including new material that came to attention since the publication of my eponymous book 20 years ago, as well as the Lee Moor Tramway and the Plymouth & Dartmoor Railway – both the latter subject of fully researched books of their own.

The locomotive information comes exclusively from the IRS *Industrial Railways and Locomotives of South Western England* 2012 (amended to 2016) for which I assisted with the Plymouth section. I am grateful to the IRS for their kind permission to reproduce the locomotive data.

SOURCES

Individual sources are quoted in each section, however the following cover the area in general:

Anthony, G. H. rev Jenkins, S. C. *The Launceston Branch,* The Oakwood Press 1997

Cooke, R. A. *Track Layout Diagrams of the GWR & BR(W),* 1984

Crosier, L. *Mechanical signalling in Plymouth,* Signalling Record Society 2000

Hateley, R. (compiler) *Industrial Railways and Locomotives of South Western England,* IRS 2012

Kingdom, A. R. *The Turnchapel Branch,* Oxford Publishing Co 1982

Kingdom, A. R. *The Plymouth Tavistock and Launceston Railway,* ARK Publications 1990

Kingdom, A. R. *The Plymouth to Yealmpton Railway* ARK Publications 1998

Mills, B. *Backtracking Around Friary, Laira and the Plym,* Pen & Ink Publishing 2013

Mills, B. *Backtracking Around Millbay, Saltash and the Tamar,* Pen & Ink Publishing 2016

Mitchell, V and Smith, K. *Branch Lines Around Plymouth,* Middleton Press 1997

IRS *Rail Cranes of Devon* (unpublished draft)

Plymouth & West Devon Record Office archives (PWDRO)

Devon Naval Heritage Centre – previously Plymouth Naval Base Museum (DNHC/PNBM)

ACKNOWLEDGEMENTS

The staff of Plymouth & West Devon Record Office (PWDRO) have endured my frequent visits and retrieved a multitude of documents from their archives; thank you for your perseverance.

My colleagues in the Industrial Railway Society and the Industrial Locomotive Society have over the last 23 years freely corresponded about many of these sites.

Cornwall Railway Society and its excellent website, with the very accommodating photographers who have contributed their work.

The local railway team of experts (though they might deny this attribute) of Maurice Dart, Bernard Mills and A. R. Kingdom who freely gave access to their knowledge, extensive photo collections and archives. Brian Moseley for his documentation of much of Plymouth's lesser known history. Many friends in the Plymouth Railway Circle.

The Superintendent Officer of RNAD Ernesettle for granting permission to allow access and use of the site archive.

Wheal Martyn China Clay Museum.

All the photographers credited, many of whom generously allowed reproduction here. For any photographs not correctly credited, I sincerely apologise.

Finally, and once again, I thank my wife Diane, who has endured my attention on this project while in preparation. To her this book is dedicated.

NOTE

The underlisted subjects were articles I authored in the specialist journals of the IRS and ILS, and have been revised and updated for this volume.

Crownhill Reservoir – IL 76 1995
Royal William Yard Tramway – IRR 146 September 1996
Relf & Pethick – IL 108 2003 (with Geoff Hill)
Breakwater Quarries – IRR 198 September 2009
North East Defences – IL 154 2015
Plympton Water Supply scheme – IRR 222 September 2015

IL (*Industrial Locomotive* – Journal of the ILS)
IRR (*Industrial Railway Record* – journal of the IRS)

Abbreviations

Locomotive manufacturers

AB	Andrew Barclay, Sons & Co. Ltd, Kilmarnock
AE	Avonside Engine Co. Ltd, Bristol
AK	Alan Keef Ltd, Ross-on-Wye, Herefordshire
AP	Aveling & Porter Ltd, Invicta Works, Rochester, Kent
B	Barclays & Co, Kilmarnock
CE	Clayton Equipment, Hatton, Derbyshire
DC/Bg	Drewry Car Co. Ltd, London; manf by EE Baguley Ltd, Burton-on-Trent, Staffs
DC/VF	Drewry Car Co. Ltd, London; manf by Vulcan Foundry Ltd, Newton-le-Willows, Lancashire
Derby	BR Derby Locomotive Works
EEV	English Electric Co. Ltd, Vulcan Works, Newton-le-Willows
FE	Falcon Engineering & Car Works Co. Ltd, Loughborough
FH	FC Hibberd & Co. Ltd, Park Royal, London
FJ	Fletcher Jennings & Co, Lowca Engine Works, Whitehaven
HC	Hudswell, Clarke & Co. Ltd, Railway Foundry, Leeds
HE	Hunslet Engine Co. Ltd, Hunslet, Leeds
HH	Henry Hughes & Company, Falcon Works, Loughborough
HL	R&W Hawthorn, Leslie & Co. Ltd, Forth Bank Works, Newcastle-upon-Tyne
HLT	Hughes Locomotive & Tramway Works Ltd, Loughborough
JF	John Fowler & Co. (Leeds) Ltd, Hunslet, Leeds
MR	Motor Rail Ltd, Simplex Works, Bedford
MW	Manning, Wardle & Co. Ltd, Boyne Engine Works, Leeds
OK	Orenstein & Koppel AG, Berlin & Nordhausen, Germany
P	Peckett & Sons Ltd, Atlas Engine Works, Bristol
R&R	Ransoms & Rapier Ltd, Riverside Works, Ipswich
RH	Ruston & Hornsby Ltd, Lincoln
RR	Rolls-Royce Ltd, Sentinel Works, Shrewsbury
S	Sentinel (Shrewsbury) Ltd, Battlefield Works, Shrewsbury
S&H	Strachan & Henshaw Ltd, Ashton, Bristol
SS	Sharp, Stewart & Co. Ltd, Atlas Works, Manchester & Glasgow
TH	Thomas Hill (Rotherham) Ltd, Vanguard Works, Kilnhurst
Unimog	Mercedes-Benz, Germany
WB	WG Bagnall Ltd, Castle Engine Works, Stafford
WR	Wingrove & Rogers Ltd, Kirkby, Liverpool

Crane manufacturers

Coles	Coles Cranes Ltd, Sunderland	JW	John Wilson, Sandhills & Birkenhead
G	Grafton, Leicester	PR	Preistman, Hull
HJC	Henry J. Coles, Derby	SP	Stothert & Pitt, Bath
J&A	Jessop & Appleby, London & Leicester	T&H	Taylor & Hubbard, Leicester
JB	Joseph Booth, Rodley, Leeds	TS	Thomas Smith, Rodley

Engine types (etc)

BE	Battery electric	OC	Outside cylinders
D	Diesel	PM	Petrol mechanical
DE	Diesel electric	ST	Saddle tank
DH	Diesel hydraulic	T	Tank
DM	Diesel mechanical	t	Tons
E	Electric	TG	Tank, geared drive
F	Fireless	VB	Vertical boiler
IC	Inside cylinders	WT	Well tank

Other abbreviations

s/s Scrapped or sold

Locomotive tables data headings

Column 1: running number
Column 2: name / previous identity
Column 3: wheel arrangement
Column 4: engine type
Column 5: manufacturer
Column 6: works number
Column 7: year of manufacture/delivery when new
Column 8 & 9: note references

Example:

Gauge : 4ft 8½ ins

1	2	3	4	5	6	7	8	9
P 402D	(08398) ANNABEL	0-6-0	DE	Derby	-	1958	(c)	(5)

(c) ex ECC Ports Ltd, Fowey Jetties, Cornwall, 7/1988.

(5) to Blackpool Dries, Burngullow, Cornwall, after 21/11/1990, by 26/1/1991.

Marsh Mills China Clay works 1961

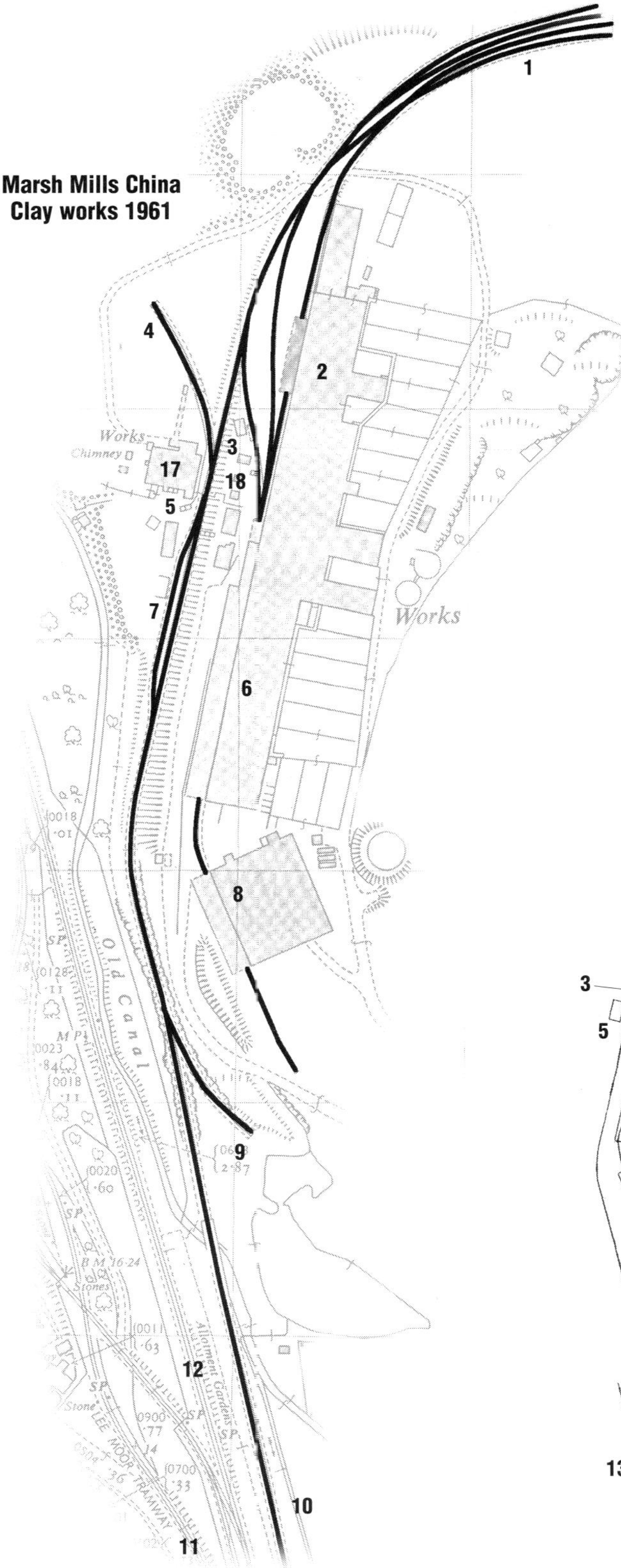

1 Fan of sidings. **2** Clay dries. **3** Weighbridge. **4** Siding. **5** Works. **6** Clay dries. **7** Loop. **8** Storage bins. **9** Siding. **10** Line to junction at Marsh Mills station. **11** Lee Moor Tramway. **12** GWR/BR line to Tavistock and Launceston. **13** Plym Valley Railway platform. **14** Clay Mill. **15** Powder mill. **16** Fan of sidings on extended line. **17** Power station. **18** Fireless loco charging point.

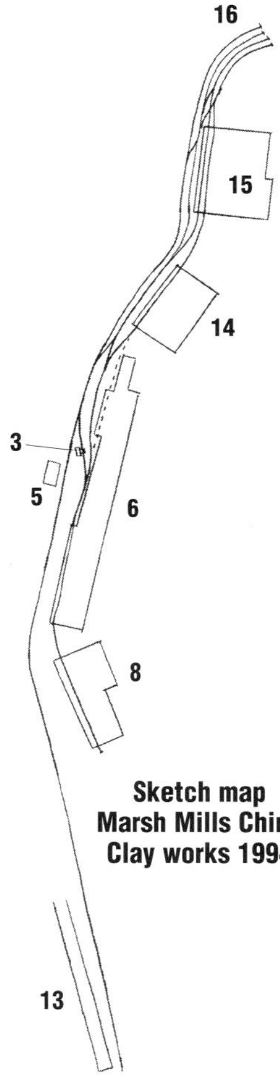

Sketch map Marsh Mills China Clay works 1994

Clay, bricks and cement

Marsh Mills China Clay Works

The discovery of kaolin in the Lee Moor area of south-west Dartmoor in the 19th century led to various producers establishing works to process the material. The Lee Moor Tramway was built and opened in 1854 to serve this industry by carrying the finished product to Plymouth. However an increase in production in the early 20th century involved moving the wet clay by pipeline 6 miles long to a new modern works at Marsh Mills, rather than processing at smaller establishments on the moor. Ultimately this led to the demise of the LMT. The Dartmoor China Clay Co Ltd constructed the works, and lay in a branch siding under an agreement dated 9 May 1919 and brought into use 7 June 1921. Sidings amounting to 1,550 yards of track were laid on fir sleepers. In addition to the standard gauge there was a 60 yard long tramway with wagons hauled by a steam winch to supply coal for the power station.

J. Fowler 22917 of 1940 on the loop siding with the power station left rear. June 1958. © IRS

Clay hoppers awaiting loading by the dries.
MAURICE DART COLLECTION

The changing face of china clay company ownership bought mergers and the formation of English Clay Lovering & Pochin (ECLP) from a number of smaller companies, which then acquired Dartmoor China Clay in 1938. The private siding agreement was transferred to ECLP on 15 February 1951.

After 1967 the original layout was amended as part of a substantial extension to the works with the addition of a new dryer and clay store. An array of four dead end sidings led into a deep cutting at the north end of the site.

The weighbridge is on the left and the line to Tavistock Junction on the right. 2008.
PAUL BURKHALTER

ECLP became English China Clays, then was acquired by the French company Imetals, becoming Imerys in 1999. The operations at Marsh Mills became increasingly unsustainable, and the works finally closed in 2008.

The site extends to 80 acres, located on the east side of the Plym Valley, accessed only from the south by road and rail. The works received clay in slurry through the pipeline from Lee Moor, then dried and refined it prior to dispatch in saleable form. Some went in bulk by rail to Fowey and Par Docks for loading into ships, some was also routed via Victoria Wharves on the Cattewater in Plymouth.

The siding originally started in the goods yard of Marsh Mills Station. However on the closure of the Tavistock line in December 1962, and the lifting of the junction with the main-line, the siding was extended over the branch trackbed on 4 April 1965 into Tavistock Junction Yard, by extending one of the tracks there and shortening others.

Rail traffic ended here on 13 May 2008, and the works have since closed.

GWR - OPERATING INSTRUCTIONS 17 JULY 1939

MARSH MILLS

DARTMOOR CHINA CLAY CO.'S SIDINGS

The Sidings are on a rising gradient of 1 in 40 from Marsh Mills, and the engine working the traffic must be at the Marsh Mills end of the trucks in all cases.

A notice board is fixed at the point marked 'X' on the sketch below, and engines may proceed up to 'X' with inwards traffic. Outwards loaded traffic will be picked up from the Siding marked 'E'. The points at 'B' have been coupled to the Catch point 'Z' with normal positions for the Siding 'C' in which position they will be padlocked, and before a train leaves Marsh Mills for the Sidings, the Porter must obtain the key of the padlock from the Signal Box, place the points referred to in the reverse position, and after satisfying himself that all is clear for the train to proceed to the Sidings, give the necessary hand signal to the Guard. The Porter will be responsible for seeing the points are again locked in the normal position when the train leaves for Marsh Mills.

When propelling wagons to the Sidings, the Guard must ride on the leading vehicle, and keep a sharp look-out. He must not detach the engine until he has properly secured the

Sketch with GWR Operating Instructions July 1939.

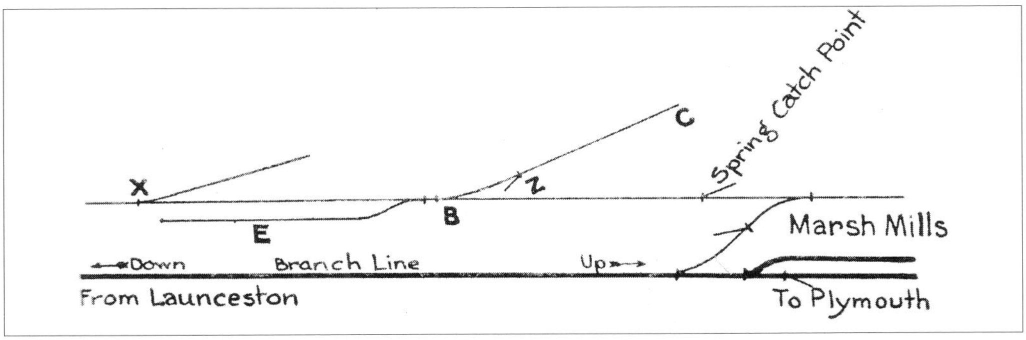

BR 57xx class 9716 on 5 February 1959.
IAN D. MARKEY

trucks. The speed of the train when being propelled, must not exceed five miles per hour, and the load must not exceed ten wagons. A spring Catch point worked by hand lever is provided for the protection of the Marsh Mills Yard, and the Guard, before closing this Catch point for the passage of the train from the Dartmoor China Clay Co.'s Sidings to our Sidings, must satisfy himself that all is clear in the Yard for the train to proceed.

BR 1993 RULE BOOK

Trains must be hauled in both directions, and must not exceed 23 SLU's [i.e. 23 wagons]. All vehicles must be fully fitted with brakes operative throughout. Maximum speed is 5mph. Propelling movements into ECLP Rotary No.15 bay must be made with one wagon only.

Locomotives - Fireless steam

W. G. Bagnall Ltd of Stafford, works number 3121. Bagnalls were a long established locomotive builder, and built a small number of fireless steam

W Bagnall 3121 of 1957. 19 July 1974.
ROBIN WAYWELL

W. Bagnall 3121 of 1957 at the steam charging point. Note the coal wagons on the power station siding. 20 Sept 1961. G. HILL

locomotives from 1924, the last of which was 3121 in 1957. Fireless locomotives have a steam reservoir that is filled from an external source and were mainly used where a live flame was not desirable, and/or where a ready supply of steam was produced as part of the site process. Marsh Mills fell into both categories, as it was required to keep contamination away from the clay, and it had a power station on site. This locomotive was ordered in December 1955 by ECLP and delivered to Marsh Mills in 1957. The loco could run for 4 hours between steam charges, and worked here until 1976 when replaced by a diesel loco. In 1977 it was placed on permanent loan to preservation and is now in long term store at the Bodmin & Wenford Railway in Cornwall.

Diesel

John Fowler works number 22917, built in 1940 and had previously

The Fowler diesel at the power station, covered in clay dust. 15 June 1957. MAURICE DART

EEV 3987 of 1970 in the sidings at the north end of the site. 21 June 1983.
ROBIN WAYWELL

worked at the Royal Ordnance Factory in Bridgend before transferring here sometime in 1948. It was withdrawn from service here in 1957, and then sent to E. L. Pitt & Co. Ltd, Brackley in Northamptonshire in 1964.

From the English Electric Vulcan works at Newton-le-Willows was purchased works number 3987 supplied new in 1970. ECLP moved it to their Moorswater works at Liskeard in February 1990.

EEV 3987 in the loop siding. 30 May 1971.
GORDON EDGAR

A former BR class 08 0-6-0 shunter, ECLP number P402D formerly D3513, built in 1958, was one of a few that ECLP acquired and has seen service around a number of their sites. It was at Marsh Mills between 1988 and 1991.

Between June and August 1987, Thomas Hill hired to ECLP a Rolls Royce built 0-6-0 locomotive, works number 10220 built in 1965.

Gauge : 4ft $8^1/_2$ ins

1	2	3	4	5	6	7	8	9
-	-	0-4-0	DM	JF	22917	1940	(a)	(1)
-	-	0-4-0F	OC	WB	3121	1957	New	(2)
P 401D	-	0-4-0	DH	EEV	*3987	1970	New	(4)
-	-	0-6-0	DH	RR	10220	1965	(b)	(3)
P 402D	(08398) ANNABEL	0-6-0	DE	Derby	-	1958	(c)	(5)

* Additionally allocated works number D1280 - not shown on plate.

(a) ex ROF, Bridgend, Mid Glamorgan, 1948.
(b) hire from TH, ex ARC (Southern) Ltd, Whatley Quarry, Somerset, 7/6/1987.
(c) ex ECC Ports Ltd, Fowey Jetties, Cornwall, 7/1988.

(1) withdrawn /1957; to E.L. Pitt & Co (Coventry) Ltd, Brackley, Northamptonshire, 1964.
(2) to Cornish Steam Locomotive Preservation Society, Bugle, Cornwall, 30/7/1977.
(3) to Castle Cement (Ketton) Ltd, Ketton Works, Leicestershire, 13/8/1987.
(4) to Moorswater Works, Liskeard, Cornwall, 22/2/1990.
(5) to Blackpool Dries, Burngullow, Cornwall, after 21/11/1990, by 26/1/1991.

A general view looking south on the last day of rail operations. 13 May 2008. BERNARD MILLS

China Clay Pits

Many clay pits in the Lee Moor area included a tramway as part of the equipment for handling the waste sand, usually an incline to the top of the familiar waste tip.

Steer Point

With the opening of the GWR Yealmpton Branch on 17 January 1898 came the opportunity for developing businesses that could be served by the railway. There were high quality clay deposits adjacent to the line at Steer Point, and the South Hams Brick Works opened a factory and quarried the clay. A simple station to serve the area was opened. Shortly after opening of the branch a private siding agreement was made dated 13 August 1901 for a siding into the brick works. The siding was operated by a ground frame. The works were taken over by the Western Counties Brick Co, and the private siding agreement transferred to them on 18 March 1929. The Yealmpton branch struggled to attract passengers, and fell to a very early demise when passenger services were withdrawn 7 July 1930. However freight continued, and Steer Point handled 4,625 tons in 1930, rising to 10,252 in 1931. Subsequent years saw volumes of between 6 and 7,000 tons. The daily goods train service left Laira Yard about 10am, and returned from Yealmpton at noon. The brickworks traffic was collected and dropped on the outward journey.

As an emergency measure in the Second World War, the line was reopened to passengers on 21 July 1941 for workmen, then an advertised public service from 3 November. This ended on 4 October 1947, with the line returning to freight only, until the line closed completely on 29 February 1960. The private siding agreement was terminated the previous 21 December.

Steer Point Station in about 1928. The brickworks siding is behind the station building.
MAURICE DART COLLECTION

In addition to the standard gauge siding, a narrow gauge tramway ran about 350 yards from the works to a jetty on the River Yealm. No mechanical motive power for the tramway is recorded here so either the trucks were hand pushed, or horses were used. This line was in use from the inception of the works, with 2,513 tons of bricks sent out, and 161 tons of coal bought in, via the quay in the year 1913. Whilst the figures for 1914 were similar, that was the end of the quay for shipments in or out, with the track probably lifted for reuse in the quarry. By contrast the siding with GWR handled 8,842 tons bricks outward, and 1,482 tons of coal inward in 1913.

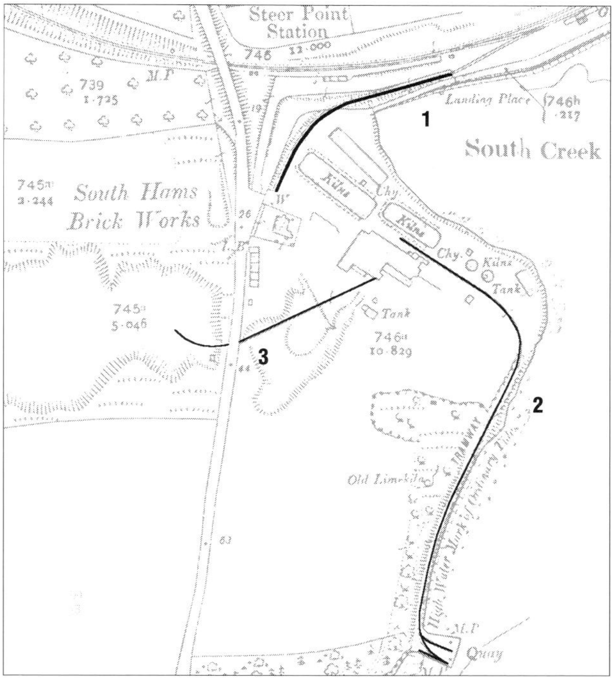

Steer Point. **1** Standard gauge siding. **2** Tramway in use until 1914. **3** 1ft 6ins gauge tramway in quarry and to works.

To move the clay from the quarry to the works, narrow gauge tramways were laid of 1 foot 6 inch gauge. A valuation survey in May 1906 recorded 250 yards in the pit; 120 yards from the tunnel to the works; all '20½ inch gauge' though 1 foot 6

Steer Point incline operation. ROY TAYLOR

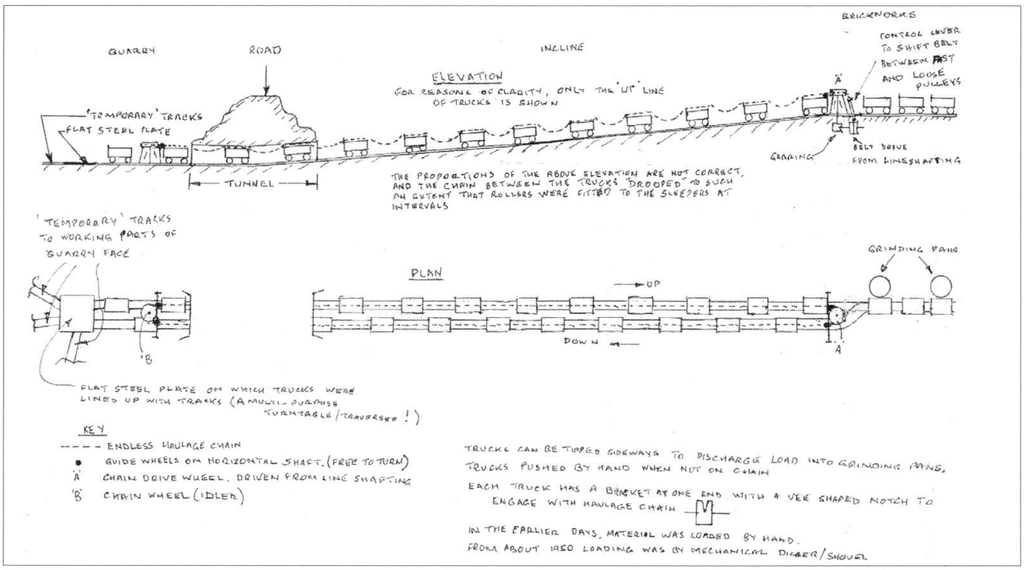

Steer Point brickworks 27 April 1969.
MICHAEL MESSENGER

inches is more likely. In the early 1930s these were replaced with a cable worked double track incline which lasted until 1953-4. Temporary tracks were laid within the quarry as required by the digging. The clay deposits were separated from the works by a public road, and the tramway passed beneath in a tunnel constructed by hand, no doubt by the quarry employees. A detailed sketch of the workings of the incline from local resident Roy Taylor shows how this operated and Mr Taylor also wrote a description of his observations in the 1930s:

> Much of the detail of this is now beyond human memory, but one line ran from the works to a quay on the river. This was used to convey bricks being taken away by sailing barge and might have been used to carry incoming coal. This line ran from the kilns at the base of the chimney stack, on an almost level alignment to a quay. The rails of the line were of light construction set at a gauge of about two feet and the wagons were most likely pushed by hand. The need for this outlet for the bricks diminished with the coming of the GWR and it was abandoned, although the track might well have been transferred to the expanding system in the quarry which provided the material for making the bricks. This quarry was connected to the works by another tramway passing under the road between them in a tunnel. The alignment from the tunnel to the works was dead straight, but as

> it was on a rising gradient, adverse to the transport of material, one must assume that some kind of cable haulage was used. In the early 1930s a new tramway, running on a straight alignment was made from a different point in the quarry up to the works. Double narrow gauge track was installed, running almost level from the quarry floor to about the mid-point of a new tunnel where the gradient to the works started. The trucks were of the standard side-tipping contractor's type but with a vee-shaped bracket fixed at the top edge of one end of the bucket. An endless chain ran around two wheels turning on vertical axes and set slightly higher than the trucks. One wheel was positioned between the tracks where they levelled at the top of the incline and could be turned by means of a belt drive from the power shafting of the works. The other wheel was situated between the ends of the tracks on the quarry floor from where other tracks radiated to the points where excavations were taking place. A truck would be pushed onto the double track section where the moving chain engaged with the vee-piece on the bucket.

A site visit in March 1969 showed some remains, and the portal of the second tunnel under the road has a date of '1930' with some track still in-situ in the tunnel floor.

The works closed in 2008, but an exploration in 2015 revealed much of railway interest, such as the GWR siding gates, and the course of the tramway to the quay. Whilst access to the brickworks site was not possible, it was said that the tunnel was extant.

SOURCES

Jenkins, S.C. and Turner, C. 'The Yealmpton Branch' *Great Western Railway Journal* No 9 p354 1994
A.R. Kingdom 1998
PWDRO 1023/150 and 1023/172
Roy Taylor personal communications 1996
Michael Messenger site visit 1969

Honicknowle Brickworks

Sometime between 1896 and 1907 a clay quarry was opened at Honicknowle, north-east of Plymouth, and a brickworks established, owned by Webber and Steadman, builders merchants and cement manufacturers in Torquay. The business was subsequently owned by the Western Counties Brick Company. The brickworks closed in 1966 as a result of new works opening at Steer Point. Connecting the quarry face and the works were narrow gauge tramways which were relaid as the

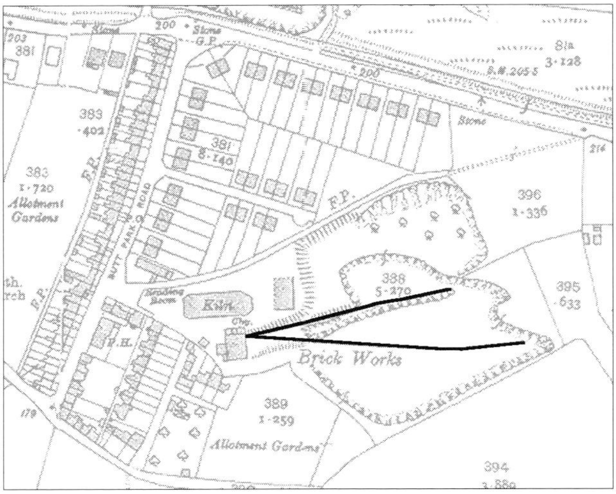

Honicknowle 1930

working faces changed. Before the Second World War the quarry face was to the east of the works, then post war the quarry expanded to the south. In 1952 either a cableway or tramway is shown serving the south quarry face. The site is now occupied by a supermarket complex.

Sources
PWDRO 1023/122; 1023/150
Website: Stone and Quarry Men of the West Country

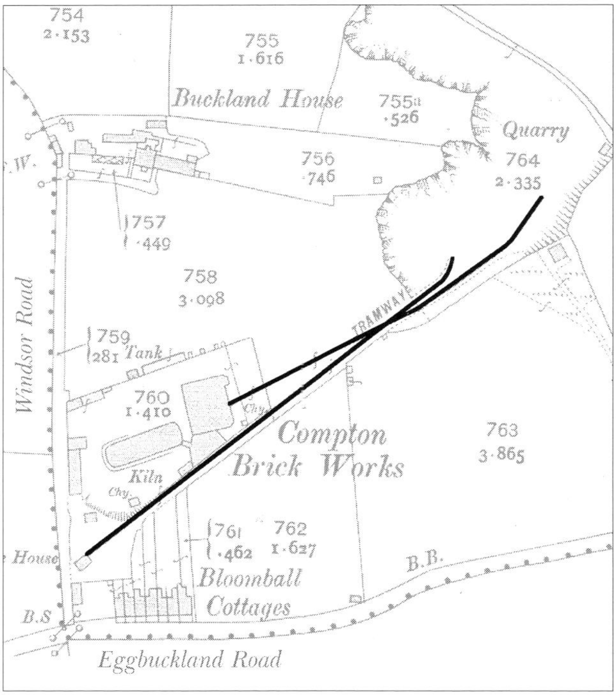

Compton 1912

Compton Brickworks

James Bros of Devonport (builders merchants) owned the clay quarry at Bloombell, Compton, and from late 19th century developed a brickworks at the top of the hill near Higher Compton. A rope worked narrow gauge tramway incline hauled clay up a height difference of 60 feet, over 187 yards of tram rails. The tramway was reported as 'gone' in October 1925. The brickworks site is extant but occupied for other purposes.

Sources
PWDRO 1023/120; 1023/150; 1023/171; 2778

Plymstock Cement Works

Aerial view in 1969

Associated Portland Cement Manufacturers (APCM, with the brand name 'Blue Circle') had wanted to open a cement works in the southwest to counter the high transport costs from plants in the southeast. In 1953 Amalgamated Limestone Corporation selected a site adjacent to limestone quarries at Billacombe, and the Plymstock Works were built and opened. They were acquired by ACPM in 1958. To increase access capacity, a railway one-third of a mile long was built from the stub of the Yealmpton/Turnchapel branch which remained after closure of the line in 1961. It was reported that 70,000 cubic yards of rock

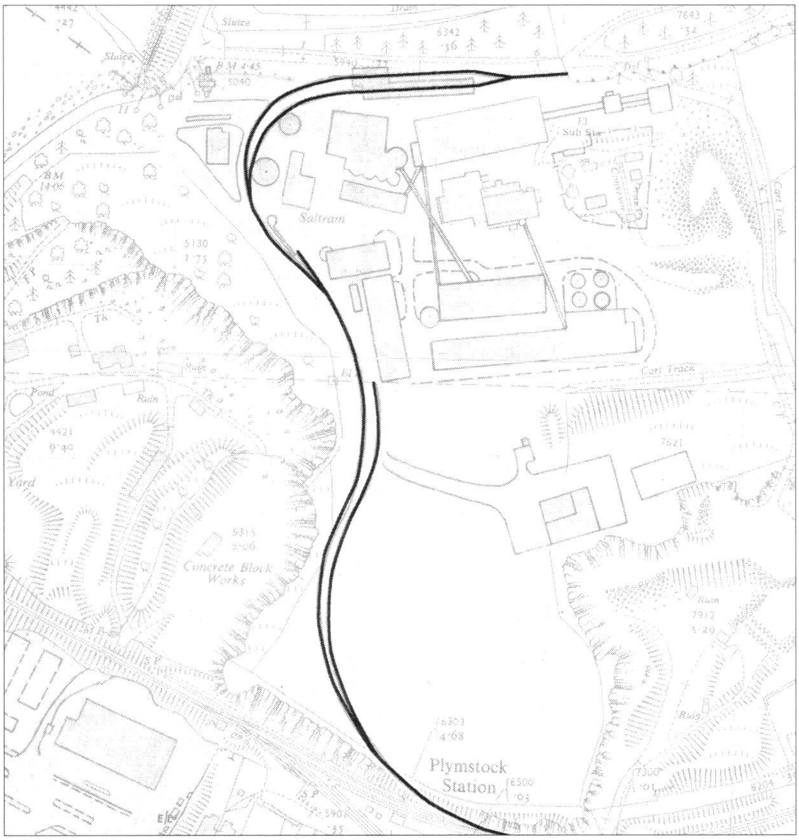

Plymstock cement works

Derailment of cement wagons on the BR section of track west of Laira Bridge with the works locomotive in attendance. 9 March 1978.
MERVYN TURVEY

was excavated to construct the new line and the track laid by T. W. Ward Ltd of Sheffield. This opened on 25 September 1963, with a private siding agreement dated 13 August 1966. To service the railway, a new Thomas Hill (Rotherham) Ltd Vanguard type diesel shunting locomotive was ordered and dispatched from the maker on 26 August 1963.

It is recorded that the works shunter was sent from the site over the Laira Rail Bridge on 9 March 1978 to retrieve a partially derailed train. Rail traffic ceased about 1987 and the works closed on 23 December 1998.

Plymstock cement works from the rail entrance.
2 Aug 1987.
ROGER SMITH CORNWALL RAILWAY SOCIETY

Plymstock Blue Circle Thomas Hill 125V of 1963. Oct 1982.
BERNARD MILLS

Locomotive

Diesel Hydraulic "Vanguard" shunter, built in 1963 at Thomas Hill, (Rotherham) Ltd, Vanguard works, Kilnhurst, Yorkshire. Works No: 125V. Weight: 29 tons. Engine: Rolls Royce 6 cylinder diesel. Power: 125hp. Wheel arrangement: 0-4-0 chain drive. Wheel Dia.3 feet 7 inches

The locomotive was acquired by the Plym Valley Railway at Marsh Mills, and was taken there on 30 March 1990, where it now operates works trains.

Gauge : 4ft 8½ ins

1	2	3	4	5	6	7	8	9
-	-	4w	DH	TH	125V	1963	NEW	(1)

(1) to Plym Valley Railway Association, Marsh Mills, Plymstock, 30/3/1990.

Haye Quarry incline. © PLYMOUTH CITY COUNCIL (ARTS & HERITAGE)

Quarries

F. J. Moore Ltd

Frederick John Moore was born on 22 July 1860 in Devonport, the son of a messenger in Devonport Dockyard. By 1881 he was a clerk in a lime works, and a lay Methodist Preacher – his family's following. He then went into the quarry business on his own account, and became the head of a large local stone supply and builders block business which lasted until the late 1950s when it was sold to ECC. His son, Frederick Herbert (born 1888), carried on the business after his father's death on Boxing Day 1924.

His quarrying activities were widespread in the Plymouth and surrounding areas, and many locations utilised some form of railway.

Deadmans Bay and Carpenters Rock Quarries (plan on page 63)

The working of the limestone deposit along the Cattewater has its western extremity at Deadmans Bay Quarry and Carpenters Rock Quarry. Originally owned by the Sparrow family, the business was taken over by F. J. Moore in about 1910. A valuation survey for Deadmans Bay in 1912 recorded 1,600 yards of track (but no gauge stated) and Carpenters Rock Quarry in 1929 records 200 yards of 2 feet 9 inch gauge tramway from the quarry face to the crusher. This site was later occupied by Plymouth Tar Distillers.

Deadmans Bay Quarry went onto have a more extensive system, with the 1929 survey recording 100 yards of 32 inch gauge on an incline, plus 100 yards in the pit. There was also a standard gauge siding that amounted to 280 yards, with another 120 yards to the Anglo American site (q.v.). The standard gauge branch reached the site through a tunnel dug through the limestone cliff from the Cattewater branch.

Cattedown Quarry

Sparrows had this in the 19th century, and in 1912 there was a 283 yard line, plus a 100 yard tram line and winding gear. This is shown on the 1914 Ordnance Survey map.

Cattedown Quarry 1914

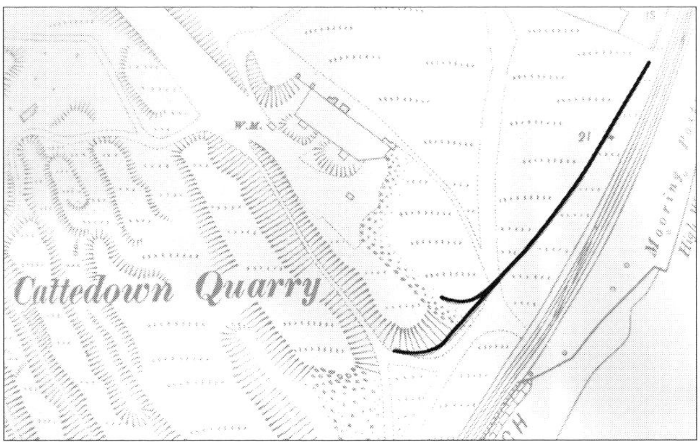

Pomphlett Quarry 1894.
1 Billacombe Road.
2 Pomphlett Road

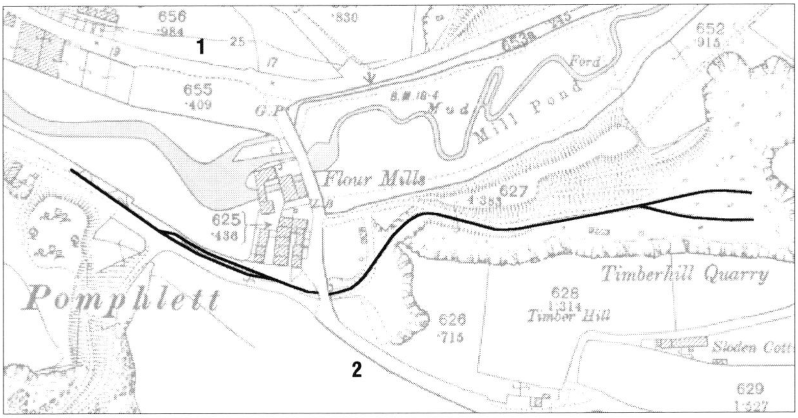

Pomphlett Mill/Timberhill/Mill Pond Quarry

(the complex of connecting quarries at the head of Pomphlett Lake)

Leased from Earl Morley to Moores, and then Wakehams from 1922. A lengthy tramway is shown on OS maps up until 1914 running from the quarry face, under the road to Plymstock, and alongside the quay in Pomphlett Lake. When the L&SWR Turnchapel branch was constructed in 1896 the embankment had a tunnel included for the tramway. For the sealing of the North Extension coffer dam at Keyham Dockyard, clay from here was excavated and shipped to the Hamoaze. In a Sale Catalogue of the Plymstock & Oreston Estates of the Duke of Bedford held on 18 July 1911, the tenant is stated as F. J. Moore, and the accompanying site plan shows the tramway extant. This Lot was sold for £1,265 to the Mitchell millers at Pomphlett Mills, adjacent to the quarry, and 713 yards of tramway is noted on the valuation survey. In the Second World War the tunnel was converted to an air-raid shelter. Morrisons Supermarket now occupies the site.

Radford Quarry 1894

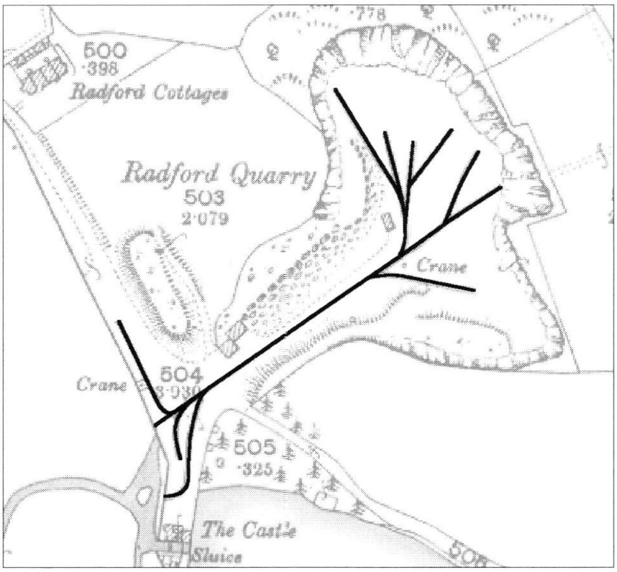

Billacombe Road Quarry

Located adjacent to the later Billacombe Station on the Yealmpton branch, there was a short-lived tramway serving limekilns sometime in the 1890s.

Radford Quarry

Located on the east end of Hooe Lake, it was opened by Gill & Co. and then passed to B. Sparrow in 1872 for stone for limekilns as far away as Morwellham. The 1894 OS shows a tramway from the quarry to a quay on Hooe Lake. In the sale of the Duke of Bedford estates in July 1911, the tenant is F. J. Moore, and the tramway is shown on the lot plan. The valuation survey in 1912 records that Moore bought the site from the Duke for £3,000, and that there were 540 yards of tramway. By 1933 the tramway had been altered from the quay to just serve a limeworks from the quarry face, but this had gone by 1967.

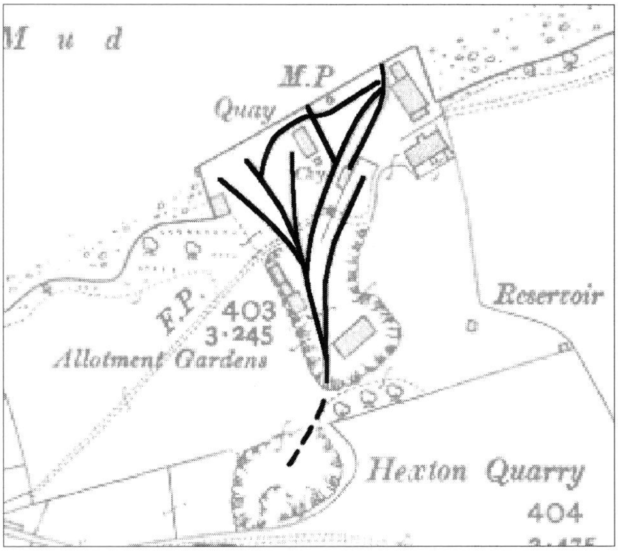

Hexton Quarry 1914

Hexton Quarry

Located on the south side of Hooe Lake, and leased by F. J. Moore, and in use before 1894. By 1906 three separate, but closely located, quarries had been linked by a tunnel, through which the tramway may have run. In 1912 there were 1,200 feet of 2 feet 6 inch gauge tramlines, but they are not shown in 1933.

Hooe Lake Quarry

Originally owned by Taylor & Wright then Messrs Sparrow. The tramway ran from the quarry to the quay under a lane by way of a bridge, which a retired quarryman stated had been built by John Hart in the 1870s. Papers with the L&SWR Turnchapel railway indicate this was in use at the time of construction of the branch in 1898. In the early 1900s there was 671 yards of 2 feet 9 inch gauge tramway from the crusher to the quay. By February 1921 the tramway had been removed. An interesting feature was that the tramway was crossed on the level by the L&SWR Turnchapel branch, just to the west of the station on the line to Turnchapel Wharf, though no mention in operating instructions is made about this.

Hooe Lake Quarry 1914

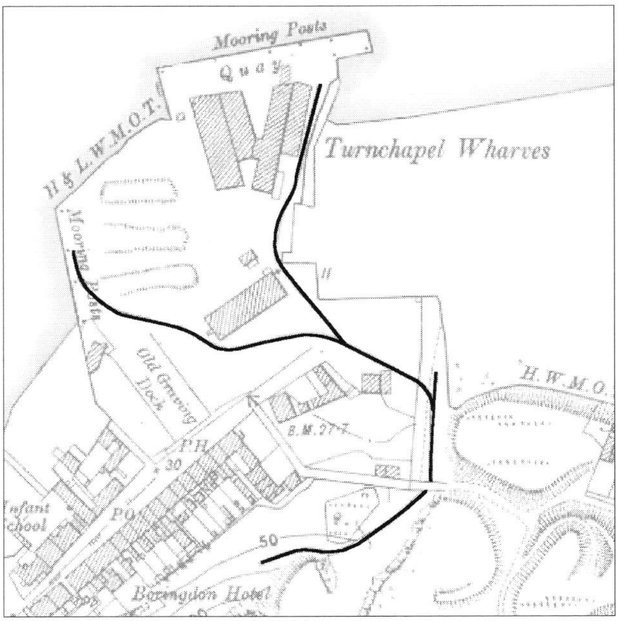

It is possible that two Motor Rail petrol 2 feet gauge locomotives may have been used here:

Gauge : 2ft 0ins

1	2	3	4	5	6	7	8	9
-	-	4w	PM	MR	1104	1918	(a)	s/s c.1946
-	-	4w	PM	MR	5404	1932	(b)	(1)

(a) ex WDLR '2825'
(b) ex R.R. Paton, dealer, Cardiff, 12/1937

(1) to ECLP, Rostowrack Works, Cornwall, 1/1949

Standard Gauge sidings

- Oreston: The private siding agreement is dated 4 May 1931, and the short siding was bought into use on 28 July 1931, located on the Turnchapel branch adjacent to the station. This was closed when the branch ceased operation.
- Turnchapel: Two sidings adjacent to the station at Turnchapel. Bought into use on 30 March 1927, it was later taken over by the Air Ministry to serve the oil tanks built on the quarry site.

THE 1960 BR OPERATING INSTRUCTIONS

These sidings which are under the supervision of the Yard Master at Plymouth Friary, are situated on the down side, and are connected with the single line leading to Admiralty Wharves. The siding connection is worked from the Signal Box. The gradient of the platform line, loop, and single line is 1 in 80 falling from the signal box to the Admiralty Wharves and attention is directed to the requirements of Rule 151. Wagons left standing

Oreston siding.
A.R. KINGDOM

Turnchapel oil tanks site entrance. 30 Sep 1961.
MAURICE DART

on the loop or platform line must be placed on the signal box side of the catch points in those lines. Wagons must not be allowed to stand on the single line between the catch points and Admiralty Wharves. Catch Points are provided in the siding connection at the clearance point with the single line. A gate, the key of which is kept in the Signal Box, is provided at the Commission's boundary. A gate, the key of which is kept by the Oil Depot representative, is also provided at the entrance to the sidings and before vehicles are worked to or from the sidings, the Shunter or person in charge must arrange for the gate to be opened by the Oil Depot representative. After completion of the work the Shunter or person in charge must advise the Oil Depot representative that the gate can be closed and locked. The sidings are worked by shunting engine. The Commission's engine must not proceed into the sidings beyond the engine restriction board situated at a point 15 yards inside the gate at the entrance to the sidings.

The Turnchapel Signal Box lever was No.2 which operated both the siding point and the catch point simultaneously.

SOURCES

Census returns 1881-1911
Hooelake.org
PWDRO: 1023/151 and 172; 1096/72; 652; 567/69
TNA: WORK 28/170
Western Morning News 30 and 31 Dec 1924

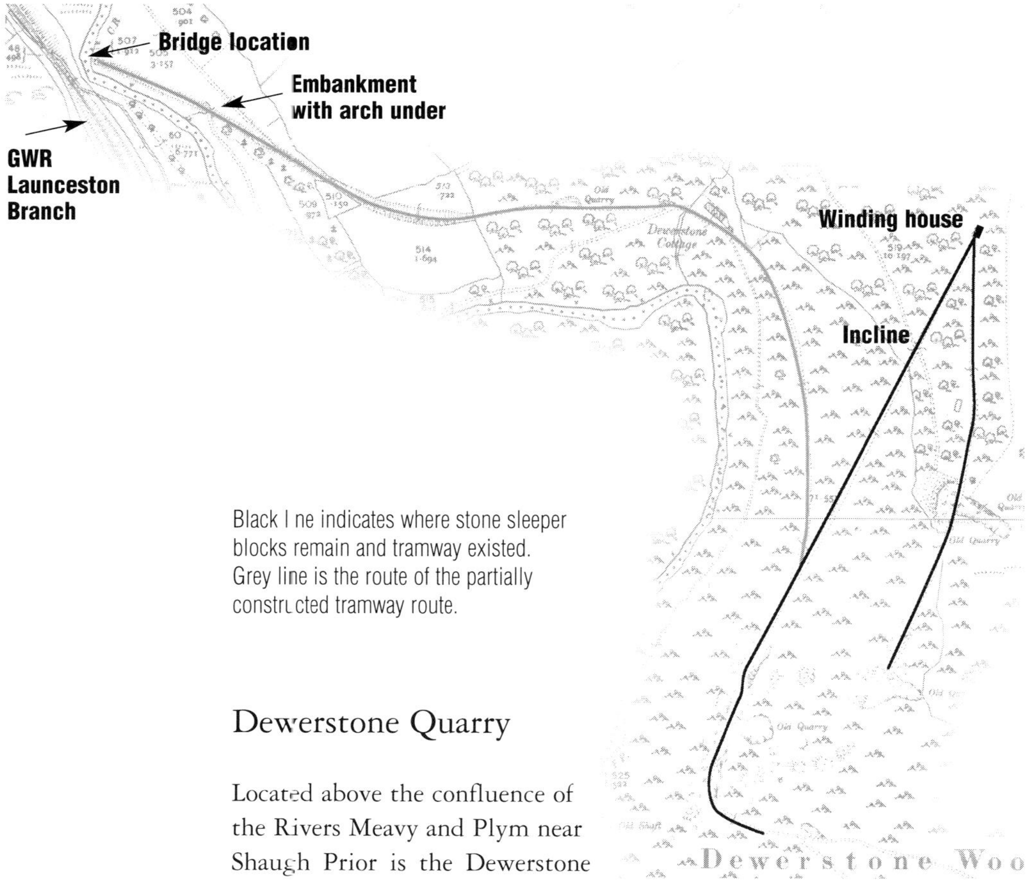

Black line indicates where stone sleeper blocks remain and tramway existed. Grey line is the route of the partially constructed tramway route.

Dewerstone Quarry

Located above the confluence of the Rivers Meavy and Plym near Shaugh Prior is the Dewerstone Rock, a prominent outcrop of granite at the southern slopes of Dartmoor. In the late 1850s, the Johnson Brothers (who had previously been working the Haytor Quarries on south-east Dartmoor) had been active at Foggintor, near Princetown, and also ran the Plymouth & Dartmoor Railway. In 1857 they began operations at Dewerstone to quarry the granite there. In order to transport the stone, a standard gauge tramway on stone setts was laid from a high level quarry to a reversing point above a rope worked incline 325 yards long down to the lower level to another quarry and dump and from where possibly the line ran down the hillside to near Goodameavy Bridge.

Dewerstone winding house remains in 1926.
F.H.C. CASBOURNE SLS

It had been intended that the line would cross the River Meavy to a siding on the South Devon & Tavistock Railway, and the landowner, Sir Massey Lopes, granted permission for this. Agreement was reached in late 1858 with the railway company, and work commenced. A substantial cutting led to an embankment under which a bridge was constructed to cross a track on the east side of the river, abutments either side of the river were built and the GWR widened the embankment for a siding. However, no bridge was installed, and no GWR siding constructed. It is not clear why this situation occurred, though Ernie Hoblyn puts forward a theory that as Johnsons also owned (effectively) the Plymouth & Dartmoor Railway, it was cheaper to cart the stone to nearby Clearbrook on the P&D, than to install the siding and pay dues to the GWR.

The incline was a single track, with a loop passing place in the middle. No locomotives are recorded here, hence it is assumed horses were used as motive power.

By 1884 Johnsons were no longer involved, and the quarries were to be advertised by the owner, but it would appear they were then defunct and records peter out.

Much remains today of the trackbed, complete with stone sleeper blocks on the higher levels and the incline. The winding house remains are extant with some of the gear intact. The embankment to the river crossing was raided for material in 1953 to build Lopwell Dam, on the River Tavy, but the bridge abutments still exist. The underbridge has recently been restored by the National Trust, who now own the land.

SOURCE
Hoblyn, E. *Industrial Archaeology of the Plym Valley* Amberley Publishing 2013

Bedford Quarry, Pomphlett

In 1898 this was owned by the Duke of Bedford, and operated by Sir John Jackson, who would have been obtaining stone for his Keyham Dockyard Extension Contract (*q.v.*). There were two steam cranes (presumably two of those noted for the Dockyard contract) and 100 yards of standard gauge track for them.

PWDRO 1023/172

Langshill Quarry

Located at the entrance to Hooe Lake, and immediately adjacent to the Bayly timber works. The 1907 OS shows it 'disused'.

Langshill Quarry

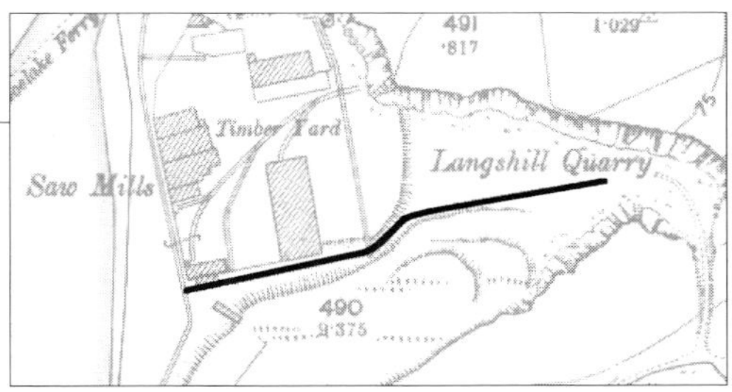

Haye Quarry

In 1933 there was about 50 yards of 'rough' tramlines. The 1951 OS shows a winch operated incline out of the quarry, with branches to a waste tip.

PWDRO 1023/149

Clovelly Bay

A short tramway serving some buildings around the 1900s up until the 1950s

Yealm Bridge

Valuation Records note the quarries around Yealm Bridge, near Yealmpton, owned by Lt. Col. Bastard of Kitley had tramways, in one quarry of 300 yards, and another 400 yards.

West Hoe Quarry/Pier

The limestone quarry at West Hoe (now West Hoe Park) owned by Thomas Gill, had a short tramway linking it to Two Coves Quay. This later ran in a tunnel under the road to West Hoe Pier when that was constructed early in the 1880s. The tunnel is still extant.

West Hoe Pier, **1** Tunnel from West Hoe Quarry.

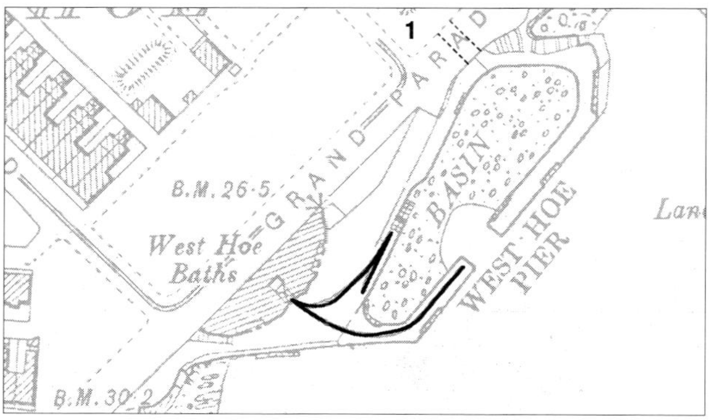

In 1877 the Plymouth Pier Co Ltd was incorporated with the object to construct two limestone jetties protecting a boat basin and to build baths in an adjacent building. This was located at Two Coves Quay, and the OS maps show tramrails from the baths building onto the pier.

Millbay Quarry

The quarry was located at the south-west of Millbay and provided John Smeaton with the stone for the Eddystone Lighthouse 1756-9. A contemporary description includes references to 'railroads' to move the stone. This was a 3 feet 6 inch gauge timber tramway.

Sources:

Liddle, H. 'The railways of Plymouth' *Industrial Archeology of Plymouth*, edited Gaskell Brown, C. 1980

Gaskell Brown, C. *The Eddystone Lighthouse*

Industry

Baylys

The Plymouth and Oreston Company was founded by the Bayly family in the latter part of the 18th century. Brabant Bayly, a merchant, lived at the Island House, on the Barbican, Plymouth and John Brabant Bayly, his son, started a timber and builders' merchant in Coxside, Plymouth. The company supplied timber to most of the local shipbuilders and by 1844 they had timber ponds in Hooe Lake, where logs for railway sleepers were seasoned. In 1875 the business was renamed the Plymouth and Oreston Timber Company and timber was imported from Scandinavia, Canada, Russia and Brazil. Oreston became the main timber yard and the Coxside premises operated mainly as a builders' merchants. All the railway sleepers for the Western Region of British Rail came from the company's yard. Various businesses across England, Wales and Jersey, including mines, shipbuilders and builders, used timber from the company. In 1919 the company was put up for sale, with a frontage at Oreston Quay of 830 feet, over 10 acres, with six acres of foreshore used as timber ponds. No sale was effected and the company kept in business until 1957 when it merged with an expanding North Devon timber merchant to become Bayly Bartlett. In 1992 the Oreston yard closed and the company was dissolved.

Coxside

The company first had premises in Coxside on both sides of Sutton Road,

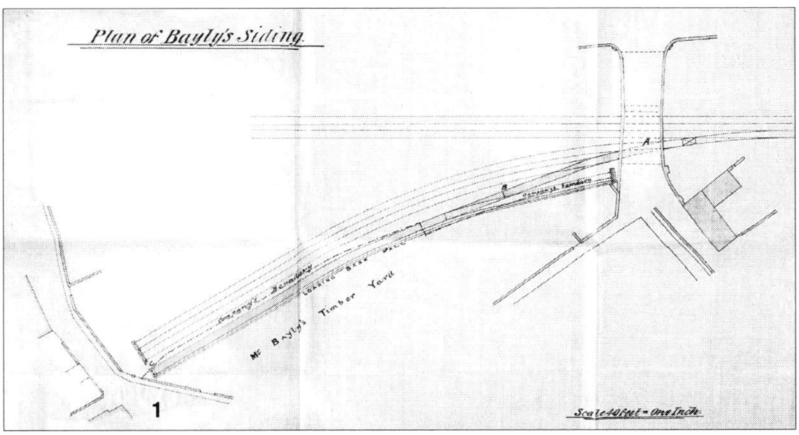

Baylys Coxside standard gauge siding.
1 Sutton Road.

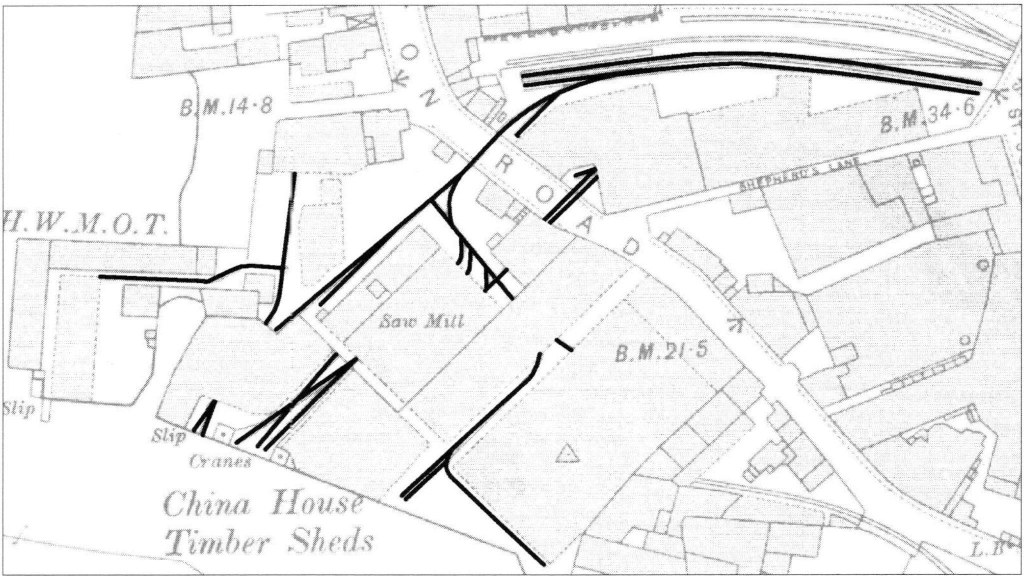

Coxside 1912

with access to the harbour. A private siding agreement is dated 13 June 1877 for a siding off the South Devon Railway North Quay branch at mileage 245¾. There was an additional agreement with the GWR dated 3 January 1879 for a headshunt siding off the existing trackwork. The private siding agreement was terminated on 31 December 1973. An extensive system of tramways (gauge unknown) is shown on the OS maps of the period, serving the mills, the wharf, and the standard gauge loading bank. These crossed Sutton Road on the level.

Baylys siding leading off left from the Sutton Harbour line. 28 Jun 1962. BLUEBELL RAILWAY MUSEUM J.J .SMITH

Oreston

The Turnchapel Branch of the L&SWR was opened on 1 January 1897, and the siding opened at the same time by a short connection from the branch at Bayly's Wharf Ground Frame east of the Hooe Lake swing bridge. The associated private siding agreement was dated 17 November 1927. The single line branch descended steeply and curved under the Turnchapel line at Bridge No. 8. The Ground Frame was released by Annetts Key from Plymstock Signal Box. The branch amounted to 1,226 yards of 'ordinary gauge' and within the works were 333 yards of 2 feet 3 inch gauge tramways as recorded in a rating book of the period.

The line enjoyed a dedicated goods service, and up until the Second World War this originated from Plymstock and ran in the mid-afternoon, then in the latter years of operation was scheduled to be two a day.

Passenger services to Turnchapel ceased 10 September 1951, and freight 30 October 1961. The last goods train to the siding was on 17 October 1961 and finally on 26 October 1961 BR diesel shunter number 11228 arrived to retrieve the sleeper chairing machine. The Plymouth & Oreston Timber Co. Board were in discussions with BR over the line

Bayly's Oreston August 1961. The timber incline structure in this image and the next was to haul timber from the water prior to treatment.
BERNARD MILLS

Bayly's Oreston 26 October 1961.
IVOR HOCKING, BERNARD MILLS COLLECTION

closure in May 1959, and once that had occurred the land was purchased from BR for £50. By 1963 the trackbed of the works branch was in use for timber storage.

LONDON & SOUTH WESTERN RAILWAY INSTRUCTIONS FOR OPERATING THE TURNCHAPEL BRANCH - 1897

SPECIAL ARRANGEMENTS AND INSTRUCTIONS—CONTINUED.

BAYLY'S SIDING.

The Points leading into this Siding are facing for Down Trains, and their normal position will be right for the main-line. They are fitted with an Annett's Lock and Key, and the Key is kept in the Locking Frame In the Plymstock Signal Box, interlocked with the Signals and cannot be released when a Train Tablet for the Plymstock and Turnchapel Section is out.

The Points cannot be moved until the Annett's Key has been placed in the Lock and the Points unlocked. After the Points are unlocked the Annett's Key cannot be withdrawn until the Points have been put back to their normal position and again locked; neither can a Train Tablet for the Section be obtained until the Annett's Key has been replace in the locking Frame in the Plymstock Signal Box.

The Station Master at Plymstock will be responsible for the working of this Siding, and when any Trucks have to be taken there, or any Trucks brought away, the Guard of the Train

A train on the branch in the 1950s.
W.E. STEVENS COURTESY A.R. KINGDOM

will obtain the Annett's Key from the Station Master at Plymstock Station and hand it to the Driver, and the Key, which has a brass plate affixed to it, lettered "For Bayly's Siding", is the Driver's authority for proceeding on to the Single Line from Plymstock to Bayly's Siding and no farther.

On arrival at the Siding the Guard will take the Key from the Driver and place it in the Lock to release the Points, and after the necessary work has been done he will again lock the Points, and will return the Key to the Driver as his authority for returning on the Single Line from 'Bayly's Siding' to Plymstock.

On arrival at Plymstock Station the Driver will again hand the Annett's Key to the Guard in charge of the Train, who will return it to the Station Master and the latter will have it replaced in the Locking Frame.

In foggy weather, before starting a Train from Plymstock for Bayly's Siding with the Annett's Key, the Station Master at Plymstook must send a competent man with two Fog Signals to be placed on the Rails at 100 and 110 yards from Bayly's Siding on the Plymstock side to warn the Driver that he is approaching the Siding.

Under no circumstances must the Annett's Key be replaced in the Frame in the Signal Box until the Train for which it was withdrawn has returned to Plymstock Station clear of the Section.

Trains going to Bayly's Siding must approach the Siding cautiously and stop Dead before reaching the Points.

A Break Van must always be the last Vehicle of a Train going to or returning from the siding.

LOAD OF GOODS TRAINS.

The load of Goods Trains between Plymstock and Bayly's Siding must not exceed 12 Wagons and 1 Van.

Sources

Gill, C. *Plymouth River*, 1997

Plymouth Herald letters 7 April 2017

PWDRO 1023/124; 2288/8; PCC/76/5/1737

Wiltshire & Swindon History Centre 2515/210 Box 30/3

The connection from the Turnchapel Branch.
W.E. STEVENS COURTESY A.R. KINGDOM

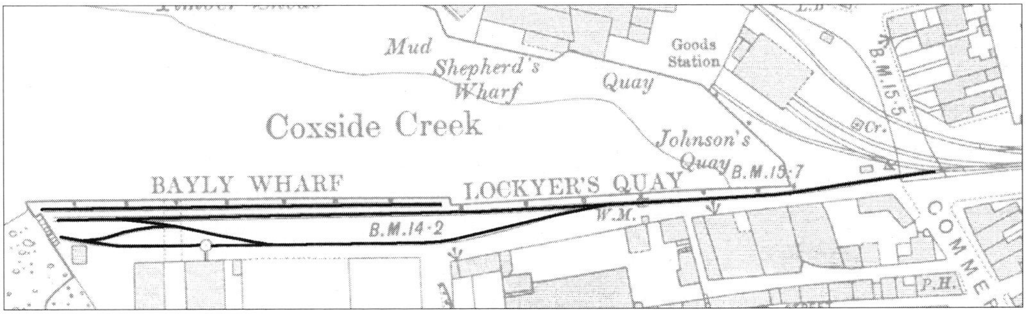

Plymouth Coal Company, Lockyers Quay and Bayly Wharf

The South Devon Railway's branch to Sutton Harbour diverged into two routes near its western end, with the southern line terminating at Lockyers Quay. The Plymouth & Oreston Timber Co. entered into a private siding agreement on 30 June 1877 for lines on Lockyers Quay. Between 1895 and 1912 this line was extended further west to serve Bayly Wharf, and the Plymouth Coal Company. This was Plymouth's main coal landing depot, with mechanical handling cranes to unload coaster vessels. A further rail and quay extension to the west occurred, post-1914, that required a sharp curve and the demolition of buildings. The private siding agreement was transferred to E. Pearce & Co. Ltd on 31 December 1960. The railway operation continued in use until the Sutton Harbour lines were taken out of service in 1973 and the Private Siding Agreement terminated on 31 December 1973. A valuation of equipment on site in December 1951 had listed a 14 feet diameter standard gauge railway wagon turntable; a 20 ton weighbridge with standard gauge railway track; and a rail mounted 5 ton Avery platform scales.

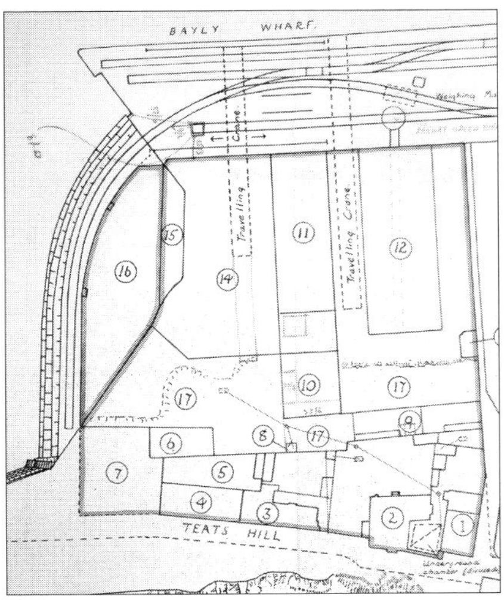

The west quay extension 9 January 1990.
MAURICE DART

A view westwards along Lockyers Quay.
MAURICE DART COLLECTION

On travelling gantries for unloading coal were two 7 feet gauge electric cranes, at least one supplied by Stothert & Pitt of Bath in 1922. Other cranes were here as evidenced in photographs and may have been a Thomas Smith 10 ton works no. 7823 of 1910 supplied to Sutton Harbour.

Sources
PWDRO 3642/144; 1908/1-2
IRS Rail Cranes of Devon (draft)

BR 0-6-0 Pannier Tank No. 1650 shunting on the quay. September 1959.
P.F. BOWLES COURTESY R. WOODLEY

Stonehouse Pool

Crossing gates at Richmond Walk with James Bros siding beyond. 1956.
© PLYMOUTH CITY COUNCIL (ARTS & HERITAGE)

As soon as the L&SWR opened their own Devonport Station in May 1876, a branch was constructed to the lower Stonehouse Pool, eventually reaching the Devonport New Quays in 1886, where the L&SWR opened a freight terminus. In 1893, in competition with the GWR, the L&SWR started running passenger trains serving the trans-Atlantic liner business for which they built a passenger station named Ocean Quay. This service did not last for long and closed in 1910. The branch then was worked as a siding, serving industries along the line, including a loop for James Bros builders merchants, and a goods depot at the terminus.

The production of fertiliser in Plymouth began on the Cattewater (q.v.) and other companies came into being as a result. The availability of water frontage on Stonehouse Pool, required for the import of raw material and the shipping of finished product, created two companies: Sulfurophosphate Manufacturing Co. and Sulfuro Fertilizers Ltd. They appear to be separate companies despite the similarly sounding names.

Sometime before 1938 Sulfurophosphate Manufacturing Co. took over the area behind the Ocean Quay station and built a factory. A siding was constructed into this from the Stonehouse Pool branch, the private siding

Sulfuro Fertilisers wharf with the two rail cranes. 13 June 1951.
PLYMOUTH CITY COUNCIL (ARTS & HERITAGE)
CITY ENGINEERS COLLECTION

agreement for which is dated 10 February 1938. At the end of 1960 the branch beyond the Richmond Walk level crossing was transferred to the British Transport Docks Board, and the last traffic was in June 1966, with the branch officially closed on 30 May 1970.

Further up the Pool, and on the opposite bank, the Sulfuro Fertilizers Ltd company built a factory in about 1941-2, with wharf facilities. There was no apparent connection between the similarly named companies. To serve the wharf two rail mounted electric cranes were supplied in 1946 by Thomas Smith, Rodley. The crane tracks ran the full length of the wharf. The company was liquidated in 1964, and the site is now part of Princess Yachts.

SOURCES

IRS Rail Cranes of Devon (draft)

South Western Gas Board, Plymstock

The South Western Gas Board constructed a new gas production plant on the site of Breakwater Quarry between 1965 and 1967, which took Liquefied Petroleum Gas and converted it to domestic gas. It was officially opened on 26 October 1967. Light petroleum distillate was delivered to the site by tankers discharging at Cattedown Wharves, or by rail to a set of two sidings laid on the site of Plymstock Station, adjacent to the

The Gas Plant sidings, with cement wagons on right. 1973.
A.R. KINGDOM

A class 31 BR locomotive with a weed killing train at the junction to the cement works. Gas Tanks for SWGB on the left. April 1984. BERNARD MILLS

line to Plymstock Cement Works. 300 tons of gas arrived by train each week, discharged from the tank wagons via a gantry system to a pipeline under Billacombe Road to the plant. Rail traffic had ended by 1987.

Lord Morley, Marsh Mill / Hoare Bros, Marsh Mills Works / Selleck Nicholls & Co

Ernie Hoblyn states in his book *Industrial Archaeology of the Plym Valley* that there was a mill here from the 16th century. When the Plymouth to Tavistock railway line was opened on 21 June 1859, which ran immediately to the west of the mill, Lord Morley (the mill owner) had a siding laid in, the private siding agreement being dated 5 December 1860. This original siding was a single line off the down line towards Tavistock Junction. The mill was leased to various millers, and from 1845 George Daw was the lessee. With the advent of mixed gauge on the branch in 1874, and trackwork amendments, the siding was altered and a new agreement was reached in 1877. The railway company had used the siding before 1874 for their own operational purposes, and had treated it as part of the main-line rather than a private siding. It therefore came as a surprise to Lord

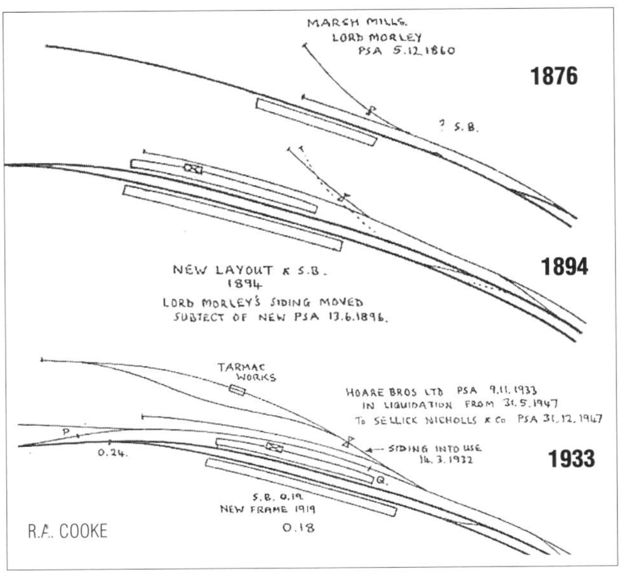

The Mills siding in general use.
A.R. KINGDOM COLLECTION

Morley when in 1895, the GWR sent a bill for repairs for £22 13s 2d. Some acrimonious correspondence ensued, where his Lordship pointed out that no charges had been made since 1878, but the GWR persisted. A new private siding agreement was issued dated 13 June 1896, no doubt to regularise the matter, with a fee of £4 per annum.

Daw shunted the sidings with his own horses if the wagons required moving after the GWR locomotive had deposited them, although Daw did object when a wagon of coal for the Station Master was left in between his wagons 'exactly opposite the mill door'.

The mill ceased operations before an auction of the premises in 1929 failed to find a buyer. However a new loop siding to serve a tarmac plant came into use on 14 March 1932 and a private siding agreement was entered into dated 9 November 1933 with Hoare Bros, a tarmac and roadstone company. This continued until Hoare Bros went into liquidation in May 1947 and Selleck Nicholls & Co. took on the private siding agreement from 31 December 1947, which continued until the sidings were shown removed by 25 October 1973. The Tavistock Branch closed to passengers on 31 December 1962, but the sidings remained in use off the ECLP Marsh Mills siding.

The 1939 Great Western Railway operating instructions stated that 70ft stock must not pass into Hoare's sidings.

SOURCE:
PWDRO 1023/171; 69/M/6

Industry: Cattewater

Cattewater Branch

Long before the 1880s the area was extensively used for limestone quarrying. Various contemporary plans show short lengths of tram lines from the quarries to the water's edge. A number of industrial activities were established here and this industrial waterfront of the Cattewater attracted the attention of the railway companies; the L&SWR sought (and achieved) a line to serve this location. In anticipation of the arrival in Plymouth of the L&SWR in 1876 their local ally, the Plymouth & Dartmoor Railway, obtained an Act of Parliament in 1875 for a number of potential lines along the Cattewater. The line as constructed was built by the local railway contractor Robert T. Relf, and opened for traffic on 3 August 1880. Many alterations have occurred over the years, with additions and final truncation. Most recently in 1993 the only sidings mentioned in the BR working instructions were Conoco, Blight & White, and Esso Bitumen.

From 2003 scrap has occasionally been loaded by European Metal Recycling, from their yard next to the line at Martins Wharf. Given that there was then no traffic beyond this point, the line was closed in 2009 and truncated at the EMR scrap site, and all rail equipment removed beyond.

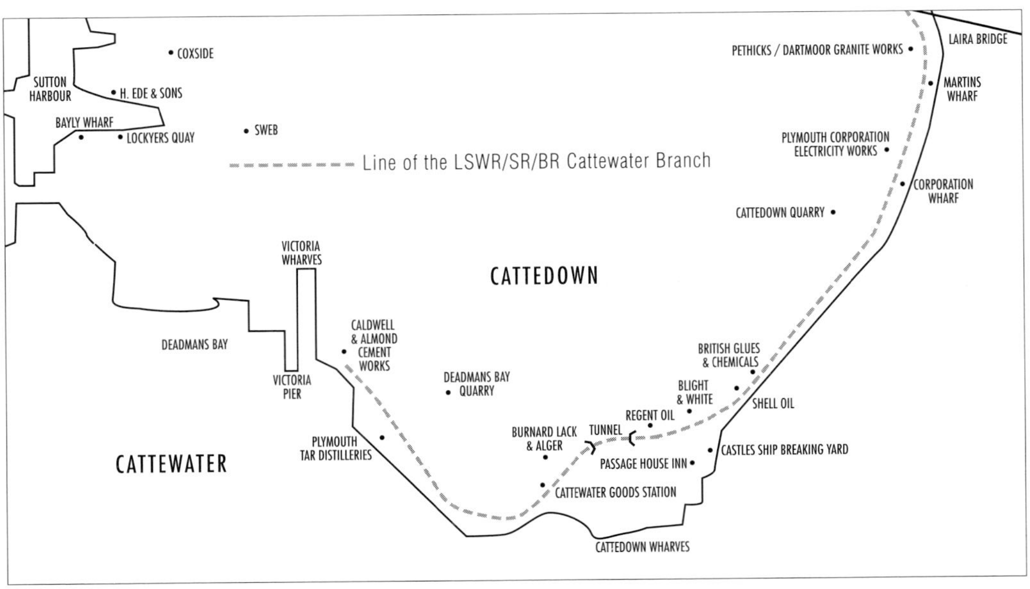

ex-L&SWR B4 dock shunting 0-4-0 tank locomotive no 30083 on the branch. 17 May 1952.
M. DALY, MAURICE DART COLLECTION

At the time of writing (2017) the remaining length of the branch is idle. This narrative commences at the eastern end, near Cattewater Junction, the connection to the Plymstock branch.

Sources
Gill, C. *Plymouth River,* Devon Books 1997
Southern Railway Western Appendices, 1934
Western Morning News 17 May 1880, 7 August 1880

The goods depot lower right. The branch continues to Victoria Wharves alongside the waters edge.
© PLYMOUTH CITY COUNCIL (ARTS & HERITAGE)

Dartmoor Granite Co / Pethicks Yard / Ministry of Munitions

On the up side of the line, opposite Martins Wharf and the terminus of the 4 feet 6 inch gauge Plymouth & Dartmoor Railway, were the Dartmoor Granite Works, owned by Johnson Brothers who also owned the quarries at Princetown and the Plymouth & Dartmoor Railway (P&DR). Branch tracks from the P&DR ran into the works, to deliver the stone blocks from the moor for working before shipping from the Wharf. The manager of the works was Richard Pethick, whose son, John, was later the contractor and Mayor of Plymouth and would own the yard.

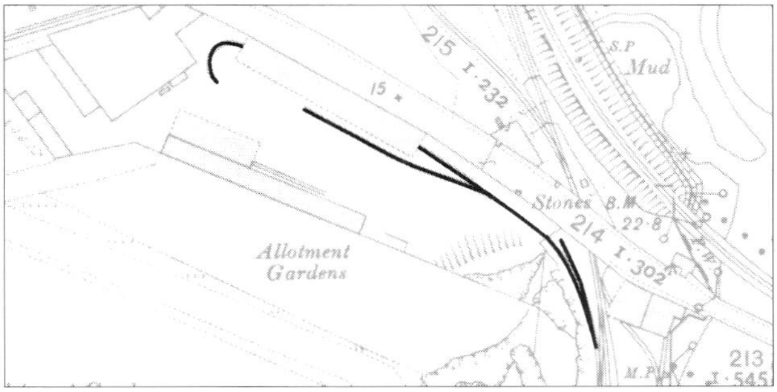

Pethicks 1914

Once the Cattewater branch was opened in 1880, the 4 feet 6 inch tracks were still in use (presumably to move materials to the wharf), as a valuation survey undertaken sometime between 1896 and 1906 makes reference that Pethicks still use the P&DR. At some point the works were reconfigured to allow standard gauge sidings to be laid. The site then became John Pethick's construction company's plant depot and works.

John Pethick died aged 76, after an accident on 29 March 1904 when his horse drawn carriage ran out of control with him at the reins in Lockyer Street, in central Plymouth. His sons continued as Pethick Bros, until the last recorded contract in 1910. In June 1914 an auction sale was advertised, on the instructions of the Receiver, for all the contractors'

E1/R 32095 crosses the LMT track with the Pethicks Siding line to the right. Martin Bros site is on the left. early 1950s.
IAN H. LANE

plant, machinery, etc, at the company's works at Laira Bridge. This included three 4 wheel coupled locos, without identifying them.

A standard gauge steam crane was delivered new here in 1891, a Thomas Smith 4wVB works number 4214 to lift 2 ½ tons.

The site then became a depot for the Ministry of Munitions (MoM) during the Great War, and a valuation survey dated 14 April 1916 records that the site is being used for storage of 'reserve coal'. This also indicated that the land at the eastern end of the site, i.e. towards Martins Wharf, had been raised and the P&DR blocked. The Corporation coal wharf was utilised by the MoM, and to move the coal from there to the yard an agreement between the L&SWR and the MoM dated 29 August 1916 permitted the MoM's six-wheel locomotive to pass from the Depot as far as the end of the Corporation sidings headshunt. The identity of this locomotive has never been established. In about 1914 a line was extended from the back of the depot to join Northeys Sidings on the Sutton Harbour branch, just a few yards away. This connection was removed by 1923.

The siding from the Cattewater branch is marked 'out of use' in the Southern Region Western Appendices dated 26 March 1934.

SOURCES
IRS Rail Cranes of Devon (draft)
PWDRO 1023/35; 1023/124;

Martin Bros, later English China Clays and English Clays Lovering & Pochin

The P&DR had extensive 4 feet 6 inch gauge sidings at Martins Wharf, at the Cattewater terminus of their line from Princetown, to offload stone from the moor onto ships moored alongside. Once the standard gauge Cattewater branch had opened in 1880 and the GWR had taken over and relaid the line to Princetown to standard gauge in 1883, the P&D no longer carried the stone from the moor. Hence Martin Bros obtained a private siding agreement dated 17 April 1899 for a short standard gauge siding of 65 chains. The siding point was operated by a padlocked hand lever and scotch block, the keys being held by the Cattewater line Inspector. Taken over by ECC from 20 December 1919, the siding was closed by the early 1970s.

Plymouth Corporation Electricity Works

Work commenced on building the Corporation generating works at Prince Rock in 1897, and the design was a pioneering one for supplying tramway

Plymouth Power Station siding entrance. 29 May 1978.
MIKE ROACH

traction current as well as street lighting. In his position of Mayor, John Pethick opened the works on 22 September 1899. A siding was laid from the Cattewater branch, via turntables, into the engine room, where the overhead crane could lift the coal to overhead stores, from which it would fall by chutes to the mechanical stokers. In 1935 the works were linked to the national electricity grid, and nationalised in 1948. Coal, and later oil, arrived by sea and rail, and lines for this traffic were laid on the Wharf after 1914, and removed before 1948. Enlargement of the Power Station commenced in the 1950s, and full power for Plymouth 'B' Power Station achieved in 1953. Sidings under a private siding agreement with the Corporation dated 18 May 1928, were extended and a new private siding agreement with the Central Electricity Generating Board dated 29 September 1955. The points were at both ends of the sidings, and were unlocked by keys held by the branch inspector. The sidings closed and the private siding agreement terminated on 20 June 1967. Plymouth 'A' closed in 1974, and 'B' put into reserve in 1981.

Corporation Wharf and Corporation Lime Works

At the outset of the Cattewater line in 1880, two long sidings were laid of about 69 chains to serve a lime works in the Cattedown Quarries. These had gone by the time the Corporation Electricity Works were opened in 1899.

A private siding agreement was entered into dated 10 October 1923 for a short siding on the down side of the line. In 1934 the Southern Railway Western Appendices noted that this siding was also used by Castles Shipbreaking Co. Ltd, a business that operated from 1920 breaking redundant Royal Navy ships on the foreshore.

Lomas Gelatine Ltd, later British Glues & Chemicals Ltd

Around the end of the Great War Lomas Gelatine Ltd, a business that had operated elsewhere in Plymouth, moved to Cattedown. This originated as a sideline to a food processing operation; the bones of animals left over from food manufacturing made glue and other products. In 1928 this was taken over by British Glues and Chemicals Ltd, which traded until the 1970s. An extension of the Corporation headshunt siding at 1 mile 6 chains, through a gate, led to the works single siding. There was an agreement in place with Plymouth Corporation for the use of their sidings. The private siding agreement is dated 24 October 1917, and was terminated at the same time as the Electricity Works on 30 June 1967.

Shell Mex and British Petroleum

On the down side of the branch another short siding was opened under a private siding agreement dated 18 November 1926 for 4-wheel rail tanks wagons. The siding was taken out of use in August 1969.

At the other end of the 48 yard long Cattedown tunnel, Shell had two more sidings on the down side, the private siding agreement for which is dated 23 December 1925.

Cattewater BP sidings. 28 Jun 1962.
BLUEBELL RAILWAY MUSEUM J.J. SMITH

Blight & White

Next to the Gelatine Works was located Blight & White Ltd, who moved their structural steel business from Stonehouse to here just after the Second World War. This was an earlier siding, said to be used by F. J. Moore, with a private siding agreement dated 25 April 1947. The siding had been removed by 1979.

Passage House Inn Siding

A private siding agreement was taken out for this short line on 3 May 1900. It was used by Castles Shipbreaking Co. in 1934. After the Second World War it was extended to link to the eastern end of Cattedown Wharves. The siding was out of use in May 1979.

Regent Oil

A very short length, and lived, siding on the up side at 1 mile 16 chains, with the points on one side of the Passage House Inn Level Crossing, and the siding on the other. The private siding agreement is dated 5 June 1952, transferred to Shell Mex & BP on 27 October 1966, and closed on 11 August 1969.

Cattewater Goods Station

Not a private line or siding, but included here for completeness, was the L&SWR/SR Goods Station on the up side. Not only did it serve local traders shipping and receiving goods, but the Burnard Lack & Algar narrow gauge system ran into the depot at the rear of the loading bank.

Cattewater Goods Station in view and 30094 shunting. 17 May 1952.
M. DALY, MAURICE DART COLLECTION

Burnard Lack & Algar (Sutton Road and Cattedown) and Cattedown Wharves

Originally located at Shepherds Wharf in Sutton Road as Burnard, Lack and Co, founded in 1854, it moved to Cattedown in 1881, and the old premises in Sutton Road offered for sale.

The business was chemical manufacturing, fertilisers and ore refining. The Shepherds Wharf site was connected by tramways that crossed Sutton Road to further premises. The sale particulars for the auction on 3 May 1881 include the statement '... together with fittings and tramways' and a site plan showing the standard gauge siding, and the narrow gauge lines from the wharf to the remainder of the site across Sutton Road. No dimensions are noted, but it would appear the narrow gauge was about 18 inches. The Sutton Road standard gauge siding was an extension of the Sutton Harbour branch into a covered way.

After moving to Cattedown they commenced the construction of deep-water wharves to ship out their products from the large factory built on a part of the quarry behind the wharf. Burnard, Lack & Algar were the manufacturing side of the business, while Burnard & Algar Ltd looked after the wharf. Standard gauge tracks were laid onto the wharf from the Cattewater branch, initially from the west only, but the wharf was extended in 1927, and after the Second World War the former Passage House Inn siding extended to connect to the eastern end of the wharf lines.

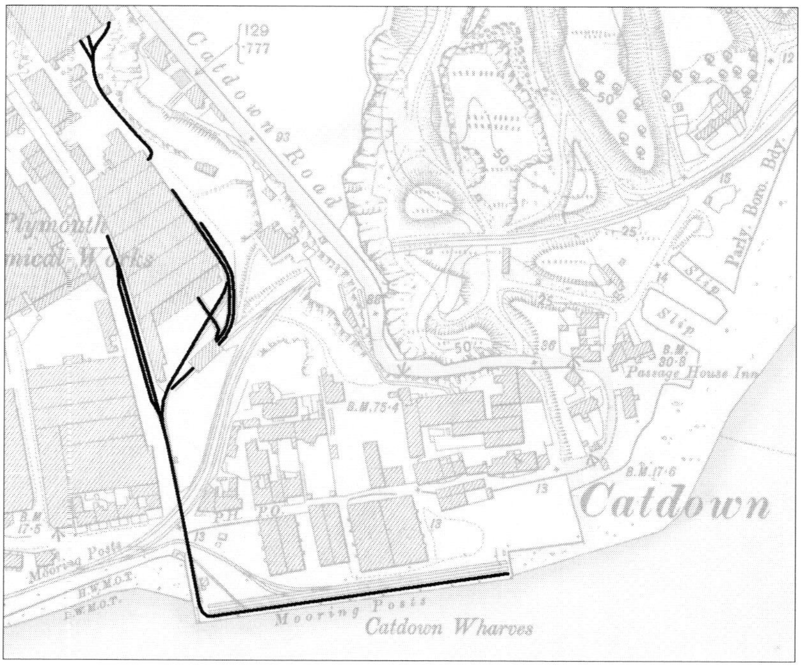

Cattedown site 1894

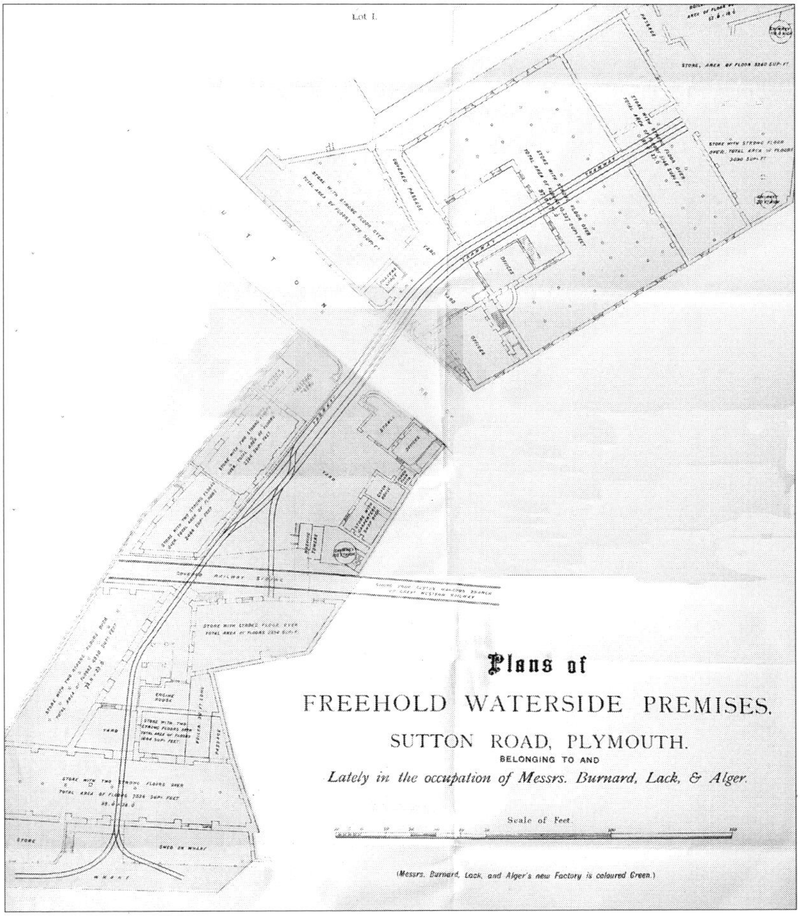

Sutton Road plan 1881

A site plan of the Cattedown factory dated 1896 shows a lengthy narrow gauge tramway system between the factories and onto the wharf. The tracks totalling 1,500 yards and ran from the pyrites burners at the rear of the site past the manure works, then on to serve the L&SWR Goods Depot on the branch before crossing the standard gauge branch to reach the wharf. Some was dual track. By the time of the 1933 OS the narrow gauge had disappeared.

Anglo-Continental Guano Co. bought Bernard Lack & Algar in 1919, and the wharf business continued as Cattedown Wharves Ltd. Anglo-Continental was itself acquired by Fisons in 1934. Fisons laid two sidings at this site with a private siding agreement dated 6 February 1940. The works were completely rebuilt after heavy damage in the Second World War, but closed in 1981.

Sources

PWDRO 274/21; 2846

S.W. Tar Distillers in the foreground and Victoria Wharves beyond. July 1982. BERNARD MILLS

HC D1363 shunting tar wagons. 28 July 1993. MAURICE DART COLLECTION

Plymouth Tar Distilleries Ltd, South West Tar Distillers, Esso Bitumen

Naphtha and tar are by-products of coal gas making, so a distillery was built to process the Plymouth gas plants output soon after 1845 adjacent to Deadmans Bay near the water's edge. Once the Cattewater branch was opened in 1880, gas companies across Devon and Cornwall sent the material to Cattedown for processing. This continued until gas ceased to be made from coal. The works were taken over by the municipal gas company about 1924. A private siding agreement exists dated 18 May 1928 for two (later three) dead-end standard gauge sidings on the down side of the branch. A new plant was built on an extended site in 1955. Esso

HC D1363 in the tar unloading siding. 23 July 1997. MAURICE DART

RR 10199 of 1964. 23 July 1997. MAURICE DART

Bitumen tanks and BR class 08 diesel heading towards the Cattewater branch tunnel. A. R. KINGDOM

took over the site after 1971, and the works commenced distribution of bitumen brought in tank wagons from Fawley in Hampshire. The first locomotive arrived in 1968, prior to that a road tractor moved wagons. The bitumen wagons were life expired in 2008 and the traffic switched to road, with the last inbound delivery on 29 April 2008, then the last departure on 16 May 2008 behind main-line locomotive 09101 carrying a 'Cattewater Farewell' headboard. The site has since closed.

Plymouth Tar Distilleries
Gauge : 4ft 8½ins

1	2	3	4	5	6	7	8	9
-	-	4w	DM	FH	3057	1946	(a)	(1)

(a) ex South Western Gas Board, Weston-super-Mare Gasworks, Somerset, 1968

(1) to Somerset Railway Museum, Bleadon & Uphill Station, Somerset, c1/1971

Esso Bitumen
Gauge : 4ft 8½ins

1	2	3	4	5	6	7	8	9
-	-	0-6-0	DH	HC	D1373	1965	(a)	(3)
-	-	4w	DH	RR	10199	1964	(b)	(1)
-	-	0-6-0	DH	S	10108	1963	(c)	(2)

(a) ex Esso Lubricants, Purfleet, Essex, after 11/7/1991, by 12/1991.
(b) ex A.B.B., Crewe Works, Cheshire, after overhaul, after 1/1995, by 24/8/1995; earlier Esso Petroleum Co Ltd, Bowling Terminal, near Dumbarton, Strathclyde.
(c) ex LH Engineering Ltd. Barton-under-Needwood, Staffordshire, hire, 27/11/2006.

(1) to East Somerset Railway, Cranmore, Somerset, 29/6/2006.
(2) returned to LH Engineering Ltd, Barton-under-Needwood, Staffordshire, 2006.
(3) to East Somerset Railway, Cranmore, Somerset, 31/8/2008.

Deadmans Bay

Quarrying (see F. J. Moore page 31)

Oil

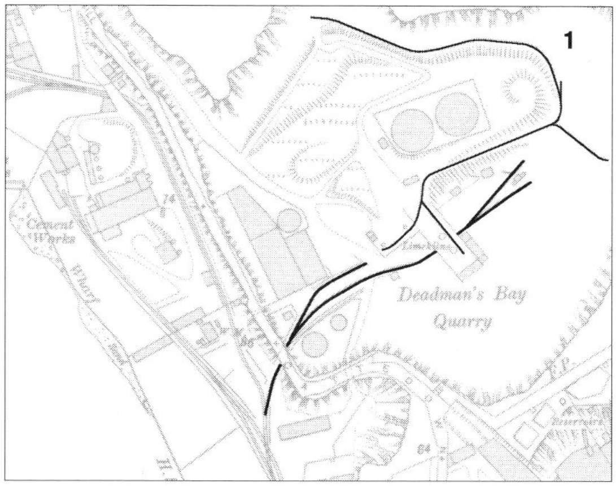

Deadmans Bay 1914.
1 Quarry tramway (see page 31)

In 1893 Anglo American Oil Company established an oil store in Deadmans Bay Quarry. In due course Cattedown Wharves became the joint oil terminal for all the Cattewater oil stores, and pipelines were laid to connect the wharf with the various depots. In 1951 Anglo changed its name to Esso. Oil products were distributed by rail from this site to the south-west of England using the sharply curved tunnel connection. The tunnel had to be raised in height when diesel shunters arrived. Standard gauge tracks extended to loading points within the quarry site. The 1934 Southern Railway Western Appendices have detailed working instructions for this location:

> The entrance to the sidings is laid on a severe right hand curve and passes across the roadway running alongside the east siding leading to Victoria Wharves and through a narrow passage cut through the rock cliff on the further side of the roadway.
> At a short distance from the entrance to the siding, hand points exist leading to three

Deadmans Bay Quarry entrance tunnel to Esso with:
Left B4 30089. 1 June 1953. ALAN LATHEY. *Right* D2134. 25 Oct 1971. MAURICE DART

Outside the entrance to Deadmans Bay Quarry. 3 September 1990.
BERNARD MILLS

separate sidings in the Anglo American Oil Company's premises, and a further set of hand points in the southernmost of these three sidings forms a connection to an intermediate siding between the southern and middle sidings. Staging exists alongside the intermediate siding for the accommodation of the Oil Company's filling plant, which staging is not of standard clearance from the near siding rail, and a notice board is exhibited near the entrance to the siding, beyond which board engines and high sided wagons must not proceed.
The middle siding extends to Messrs. F. J. Moore's lime kilns and quarries.
Shunting operations are carried out in charge of a competent man deputed by the Inspector at Cattewater.
Owing to the severe nature of the curve at the entrance to the sidings, and the difficulty of obtaining a clear view of the sidings from that point, it is necessary that movements into the sidings should be carried out with the utmost care, and the competent man in charge of shunting operations must satisfy himself before making movements into the siding that the line is clear to the point to which such operations are required to proceed.

Conoco was another company that operated from this location in 1972. A siding from the Cattewater branch was laid in, but was removed by 1979.

Sources
PWDRO 1023/188

Caldwell & Almond

As built in 1880 the Cattewater branch ended at the cement works of Caldwell & Almond. This firm had been operating in Plymouth since 1850, and were a significant supplier in the area – all of the cement for Burrator Reservoir was supplied from here. However by the 1920s the works ceased production. Two dead-end sidings served the works.

Victoria Wharves

Victoria Wharves are located on what was formerly Marshall's ship breaking yard and Marine Field, both of which were acquired in the 1890s by Cornelius Laskey Duke, a local contractor. When purchased, the site amounted to 4½ acres. To the west of it was a Corporation wharf and to the east was the cement works of Messrs Caldwell and Almond, as well as the end of the Cattewater branch – no doubt an incentive to build there. Construction was underway in the period between 1893 and 1900. Named in honour of the Queen, it was also known as Duke's Wharf.

The part containing the deep water tidal dock and the eastern wharf was leased to the Chatterley and Whitfeld Colliery Company and was officially opened by Mr T. Bulteel, chairman of the Cattewater Commissioners, on 7 March 1898. A depot for distributing coal brought in by the Company's steamers was erected, where 15 cwt tub wagons were loaded in the ship's hold then lifted out onto an overhead gantry for tipping onto storage dumps. The wagons were 2 feet gauge and there were

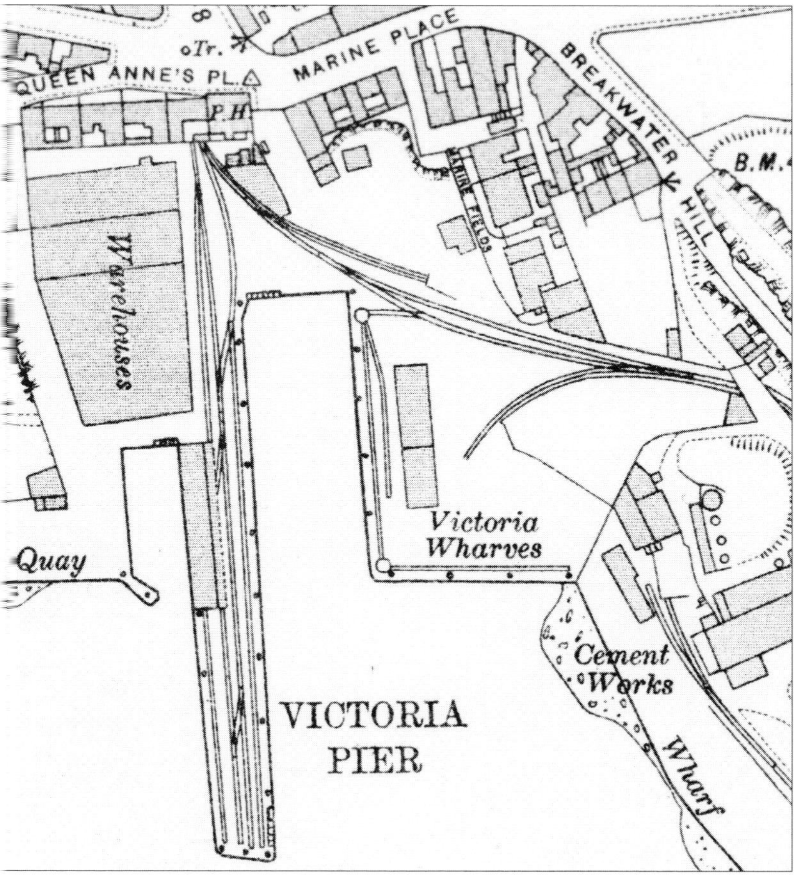

Victoria Wharves 1914.
Caldwell & Almond Cement Works lower right.

A pre WW2 picture with a collection of period wagons on the west wharf.
VICTORIA WHARVES LTD

280 yards of track on the boarded gantry. Later, John Westcotts undertook the coal business.

Victoria Wharves was an instant success. Timber, coal, granite from Merrivale on Dartmoor (some of which was cut on the quay before shipment), petroleum, frozen meat and strawberries were examples of the traffic handled. Some 4,500 rail trucks were dealt with each year. However Duke became bankrupt, and in 1914 it became Victoria Wharves Ltd, which changed its name to Coast Lines Ltd in 1917. The US Navy took over the wharf between 1917 and 1919, but when they had gone, business flourished again. After the Second World War coastal shipping faded in the face of road transport, and Coast Lines sold the premises to Bethel Gwyn in about 1977, who then sold on to Inchcape and passing to Marine Developments in 1994.

In 1948 Victoria Wharves started handling china clay and this proved to be the stalwart traffic for many years.

The wharves were rail connected from the outset, the private siding agreement being dated 3 February 1898 'whereas the said Cornelius Laskey Duke is about to construct a pier and quay… and it would be of mutual advantage that a railway or siding should be made in connection with the Cattewater Branch Line'. Duke was to acquire the land and provide the materials for the line, which the L&SWR would lay and maintain. Initially the connecting track ran between the cement works and the cliff. This latter proving to be a problem with falling rock, so a mesh grid was erected over the railway to protect it. The limited space available at the head of the dock meant that a headshunt was in a 90 feet long tunnel under buildings and a road. In 1908 a survey recorded 947 yards of goods lines; 467 yards of mixed gauge; 50 yards of crane (i.e. broad gauge) rails. In 1928 the Southern Railway undertook works to

Track relaying. Note the contractors mess coach. 5 Apr 1961.
VICTORIA WHARVES LTD

rearrange the lines and junctions at the entry to the Wharves together with the relocation of the weighbridge.

Later (before 1934) the cement works had closed, and the two dead-end sidings therein extended into Victoria Wharves. Given the amount of traffic being handled this must have been a great help, and inbound traffic used the former cement works lines, and the lines next to the cliff were for outbound traffic.

After completion of the relaying. Note FH 1834 shunting.
28 Jun 1961.
VICTORIA WHARVES LTD

For loading and unloading ships broad gauge steam cranes were introduced, with dual gauge track laid on the quaysides. As late as 1961 new dual gauge trackwork was being installed.
The 1934 Southern Railway Western Appendices are extensive:

Victoria Wharves sidings.—These two sidings form the terminal point of the Cattewater Branch, the Company's boundary being indicated approximately by a wall, office and weighbridge, the property of Messrs. Coast Lines Limited, who are the wharf owners.
Hand points situated approximately 100 yards on the Cattewater Junction side of the boundary, lead out of the west road of the Company's terminal loop, and serve the east siding leading to Victoria Wharves. The west siding is an extension of the loop road.
An overhead conveyor is provided over the loop roads, at the Cattewater Junction end at Victoria Wharves, and a chute which is operated by Messrs. John Westcott Ltd., is attached to the conveyor and, when lowered, fouls both the construction and load gauges.
Before movements are made by the Company's engine and vehicles over the right hand loop road, the Shunter in charge must obtain an assurance from Messrs. Westcott's Foreman, that the conveyor will not be set in motion over the sidings during the progress of the shunting movement.
Ingoing wagons for Victoria Wharves will usually be placed by the Company's engine on the east siding.
Outgoing wagons will usually be accepted on the west siding immediately inside the boundary gate.
The Company's engine may proceed into the west siding for a distance of 30 yards on the right-hand loop road.
Shunting operations will be in charge of a competent man, deputed by the Inspector at Cattewater, and no movements on to the east or west sidings must be made until the competent man has satisfied himself that the line is clear and has come to an understanding with the wharf owners' employees in regard thereto.

Alicie HE 366 of 1886 photographed in the 1920s.
VICTORIA WHARVES LTD

FH 1834 c1956.
M. DALY, MAURICE DART COLLECTION

The wharf owners' private locomotives are employed in the sidings and on the wharves for the purpose of making internal shunt movements, and such locomotives may be allowed to proceed from the west siding on to the Company's property for a short distance towards the terminal loop, if the line is clear, up to a point where a notice board is fixed. The wharf owners' private locomotives must not proceed from the east siding on to the Company's property beyond the boundary gate.

FH 3281 and a line of trucks.
VICTORIA WHARVES LTD

FH3281 on the east wharf. 14 January 1992. GORDON EDGAR

On the evening of 29 August 1944 the SR locomotive was drawing a loaded train out of the wharves when a truck derailed and damaged the weighbridge. It took until April 1947 for the two parties to agree on £48 in settlement of the repairs.

In January 1946 it was being noted that a possible new tenant for Queens Annes Battery (to the west of the Victoria Wharves site) was looking at how rail access could be arranged and SR officials had visited the site and agreed that a connection could be made. However it would have greatly inconvenienced Victoria Wharves and in the event was never proceeded with.

Rail traffic came to an end about 1991. In 1994 investigations were conducted to see if clay could be returned to rail, but English China Clays preferred to use Par or Fowey with the existing specialist facilities there.

Locomotives

It is possible that the Hunslet locomotive *Alicie*, was previously used by the contractors R. T. Relf who built the Cattewater branch, and may have come to the site through that connection at the opening.

Gauge : 4ft 8 ½ins

1	2	3	4	5	6	7	8	9
-	ALICIE	0-4-0ST	OC	HE	366	1886	(a)	s/s c.1935
	BARRY	0-4-0ST	OC	AB	687	1891	(b)	s/s
	-	4w	PM	FH	1834	1933	New	s/s /1956
	C.L.S.	4w	DM	FH	3281	1948	New	(1)

(a) earlier Pethick Bros, Blagdon Reservoir (Bristol Corporation) contract, Somerset, until at least 8/1900 (here by 11/1917).

(b) ex ? , by 6/1932; earlier Sir John Jackson, Simonstown Naval Base contract, South Africa, 1906.

(1) to Plym Valley Railway Association, Marsh Mills, 22/11/1993.

Note that an 0-4-0T by Gilkes, Wilson was offered for sale by auction here on 5/11/1909; it is assumed that this was one of GW 107 or 131 earlier at Devon Great Consols Ltd, possibly after use by J.C. Lang (in Cornwall) and/or C.L. Duke, contractor, of Sutton Road, Plymouth.

Cranes

Mixed gauge track (standard & broad gauges) was laid on the quaysides to allow rail cranes to operate. A complete relaying of the trackwork in 1961 included complex turnouts for the two gauges.

Gauge 7ft 0in

1	2	3	4	5	6	7	8	9
-	-	4w	VB-5t	G	395	1896	(a) (b) s/s	-
-	-	4w	VB-10t	G	693	1901	new (b)	-
-	-	-	3t	JW	-	-	(b)	-
-	-	-	3t	JW	-	-	s/h (b)	-
-	-	-	2t	JW	-	-	s/h (b)	-
-	-	-	2t	J&A	-	-	s/h (b)	-
-	-	4w	E	-	-	-	-	-
-	-	4w	E	-	-	-	-	-
-	-	4w	E	-	-	-	-	-

(a) ex Brixham U.D.C.

(b) as per 1908 valuation survey

Sources

Alex Bettany; Bob Darvill; Robin Weywell, (IRS)
PWDRO 1023/192
Victoria Wharves Ltd

The very rusty remains of a turnout on the Breakwater. 23 September 2011. PAUL BURKHALTER

Military

Plymouth Breakwater tramways

In 1806 the Admiralty invited John Rennie (1761-1821) to design a possible breakwater for the protection of Plymouth Sound and providing a safe anchorage for the ships approaching Devonport Dockyard and Naval Base. The final plan was to build an island structure 5,100 feet long, 250 feet wide at the base and 45 feet wide at the top, some 2 miles distant from the Hoe. Approval was given in 1811, and a 25 acre site at an existing quarry at Oreston was leased from the Duke of Bedford to quarry limestone for the work.

The first quarried blocks were dropped into the Sound on 12 August 1812, and this process used ship mounted rail wagons to transport the stone directly from quarry face to the breakwater site. 10 ships were purpose-built in Devonport Dockyard for carrying the rock to the site, over 3 miles from the Quarry. These ships carried 16 blocks of 5 tons each, each block carried by a rail wagon on two tracks on the deck. The wagons was hauled from the quarry face by horses, turned on a plate turntable, and loaded onto the ship, berthed stern-to at the quarry quay with a 'drawbridge' laid from shore to ship. At the breakwater site a 'typing' (or tipping) frame was used to discharge the stones off the wagons over the

Rails on the breakwater under construction. c1829.
PAUL BURKHALTER COLLECTION

The rail truck carrying ship delivering stone for the construction of the Breakwater from Oreston.

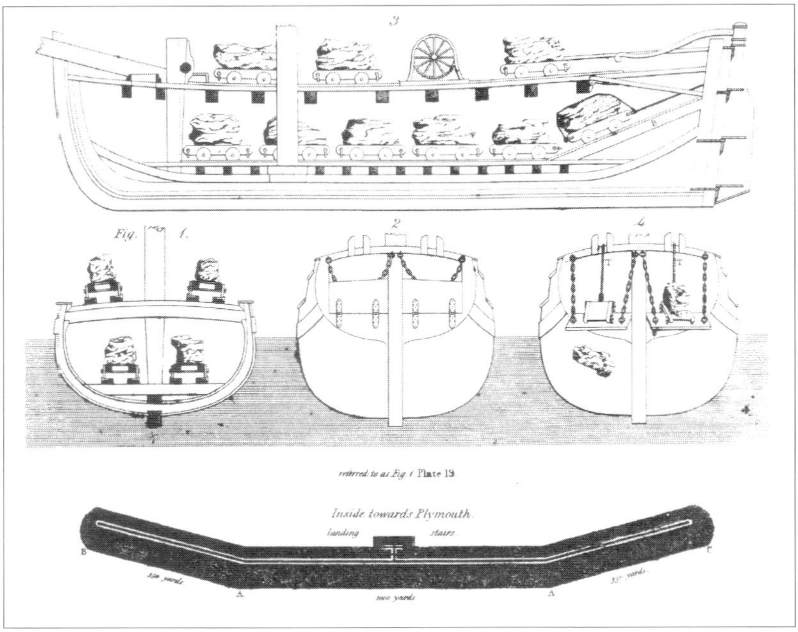

stern of the vessel. The wagons were four wheel and either flat (for the very large blocks), or with sides for the smaller rocks.

In September 1812 the local newspaper reported that a quay at the quarry collapsed taking all the 'railroads' with it. The correspondent blamed poor workmanship for the incident. Richard Trevithick visited the works at this time and was scathing about the arrangements. He built what is believed to be a self-propelled crane for the work but it is not known whether it reached Plymouth.

Despite this setback work progressed and the first sight of the stones appearing above the water was on 31 March 1813, and by the time the breakwater was mostly complete in 1841 some 3,600,000 tons of stone had been placed. John Rennie died in 1821, and his son Sir John continued the work.

As the breakwater became complete, and to finish off the structure, rail tracks were laid on the surface structure, together with turntables. Unloading the wagons became a reverse process to that at the quarry quay. A drawing survives clearly showing this track. The gauge of these early lines was 3ft 6in and horses provided the motive power.

On the Breakwater in 2011 were the remains of very rusty edge rail tracks, 44½ inch gauge, at the eastern end for approximately 200 yards with one turnout. Ordnance Survey maps from 1907 to 1951 show a travelling crane at this location.

By 1867 the first detailed Ordnance Survey map of the Oreston Quarries shows a network of parallel tracks from the inland quarry face to

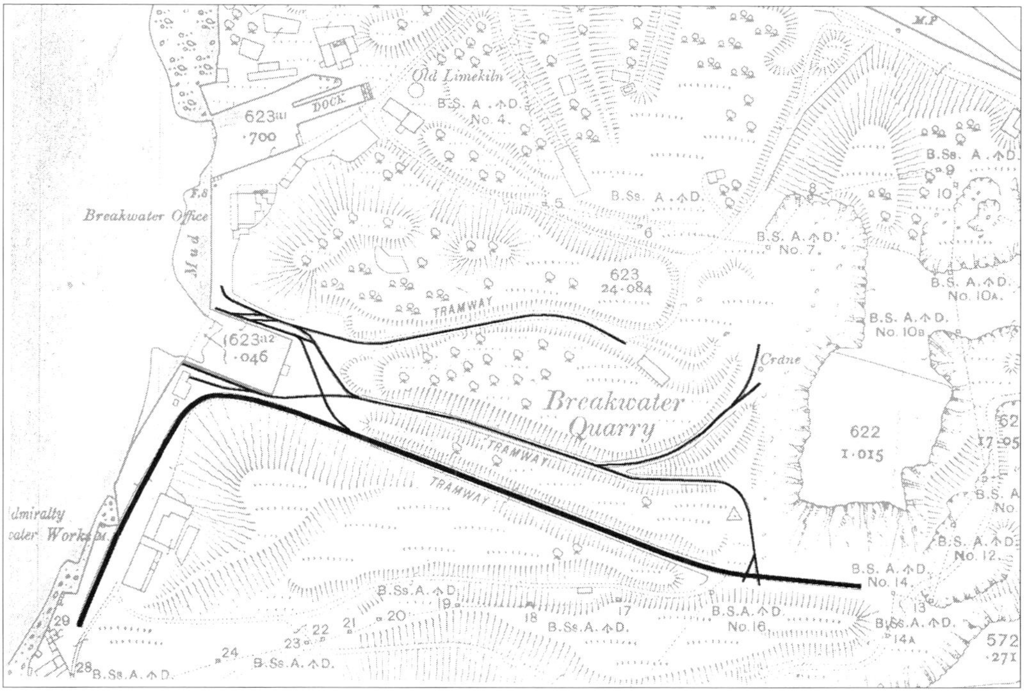

Breakwater Quarry 1914

the quay. No doubt the tracks followed the quarry face as it developed. These narrow gauge tracks remained in use until the 1960s.

From 1907 onwards the OS shows a single wider gauge line from the quarry face to the quay. Logic dictates it is 7 feet ¼ inch i.e. GWR broad gauge. The Dockyard had by this date removed all its broad gauge tracks and it could be possible that the redundant material was reused at Oreston. The wider gauge, common for harbour railways, allowed larger sized stone blocks to be handled.

The broad gauge crane track from the quarry. 17 April 1959.
STEWART BLENCOWE COLLECTION

Fan of tracks at the quarry face. 22 September 1946.
L.E. COPELAND
COURTESY WILD SWAN PUBLICATIONS LTD

The Admiralty continued to own and operate the Breakwater Quarry at Oreston up until 1967, when the site was sold and a gas making plant erected.

22 September 1946.
L.E. COPELAND
COURTESY WILD SWAN PUBLICATIONS LTD

Another tramway was located at the breakwater. In the latter years of the 19th century, a torpedo system was installed for the defence of the western entrance of Plymouth Sound at Pier Cellars on the Cornish coast at Cawsand. At about the same time a 'torpedo pier' was built on the inner side of the eastern end

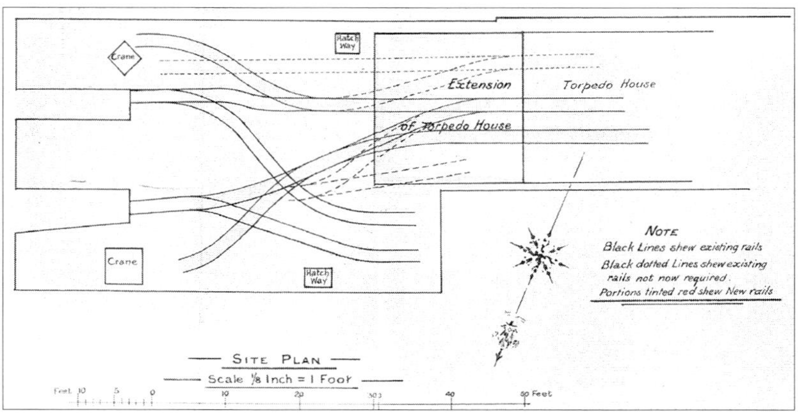

A torpedo station was built on the Breakwater with tramways to move the weapons. 1919.

of the breakwater, and short 1 foot 10 inch gauge tramway laid from the building to the launching locations. The layout was amended in 1909, and the structure lasted for some years.

SOURCES

Babcock Marine (formerly DML) at Devonport Dockyard.

Dickinson, H. W. and Titley, A. *Richard Trevithick,* Cambridge 1934

Wild Swan Publishing and Gloucestershire Archives Copeland collection (cat. ref: D5749/433/1-4).

The Queen's Harbour Master is thanked for special permission to land (the Breakwater is MoD owned and a Designated Place with access prohibited)

Canadian Forestry Corps – Plym Bridge

In the Great War, the success of German U-boats against Allied shipping in the Atlantic caused the flow of timber (and other supplies) to be severely constrained. In February 1916 the British Government requested assistance from Canada in developing a supply of timber within the UK and France, and Canadian Forestry Battalions were raised in April 1916. These Battalions were merged to form the Canadian Forestry Corps (CFC) in October 1916. The Corps remained in operation until the end of the War in 1918, with a maximum of 31,000 men in Europe.

Many sites around the UK were established for the winning of timber from existing forests and woodland, for the manufacture of a wide range of products, such as sleepers, mine props, buildings, and other items.

The 134 Company CFC, was organised in December 1917 under the command of Major C. E. King, and dispatched to Plym Bridge to work the woods in the valley on both sides of the river. The diaries of the unit have survived and provide a detailed insight of operations.

By January 1918, three officers and 30 men were on site setting up the camp located on flat ground to the south of Plym Bridge between the River Plym and the GWR Tavistock branch. The latter was inspected for the creation of a siding to hold 15 wagons, and on 21 January a meeting was held with the GWR and the Board of Trade in London with a view to constructing a siding from the branch at 1 mile 20 chains. The location of the siding was partly on the trackbed of the Cann Quarry tramway that was realigned when the GWR branch was built in 1859. Very quickly the turnout and sufficient length of siding was in place for a train of trucks to arrive at noon on the 1 February carrying material for the Unit. However it was not until the 16 April that the GWR advised the Board of Trade that the works were complete ready for inspection, which was conducted

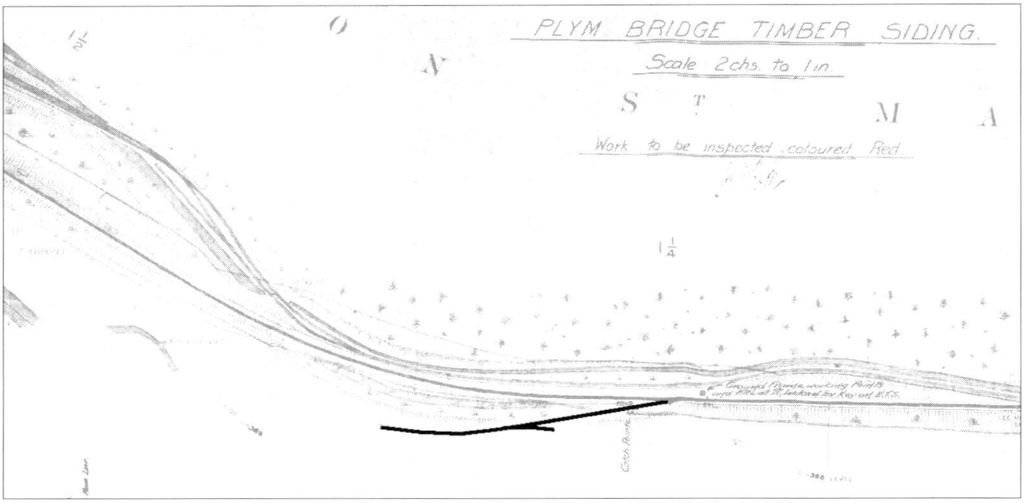

GWR plan of the siding dated 14 April 1918. TNA MT 6/2494/11

in August. On 30 August the Board of Trade wrote to the GWR giving approval of the new works, rather belatedly as the first use was in February! A two lever ground frame was released by a key on the electric staff section from Marsh Mills to Bickleigh. Trains were propelled from Marsh Mills.

As the Lee Moor Tramway was adjacent to the working areas, it was proposed to utilise that as well. Whether this actually took place is not recorded.

For access to the cutting areas, a 3 foot gauge tramway of about one mile in length was laid down in June 1918, and later extended to the furthest part of Cann Wood in September. Rail material for the tramway was arriving as early as 8 January, but was having to be stored in Plymouth until the siding was ready. German prisoners of war were employed on various tasks including rail track laying.

Motive power was horse haulage, for which forage was delivered by rail. 49 heavy duty horses were recorded on site in March 1918

With the end of the war in November 1918 activities were run down with cutting ceasing in January 1919, and the site cleared in February. The operation produced a total of 321,000 cubic feet of timber.

It is reported that the siding reopened on 13 July 1922 for a short period for the loading of timber. The subsequent re-closure is not recorded.

SOURCES:

Library and Archives of Canada, RG 9 III-D3, vol 5018; 134Co. CFC Diary

TNA, MT 6/2494/11

Devonport Dockyard

Admiralty (later Ministry of Defence), and contractors.

The origins of the Dockyard date from 1690 when a dock was constructed on this site, now No. 1 Dock in South Yard. The facilities grew over the ensuing centuries until the advent of steam propulsion and machinery in the mid-19th century. Along the way minor use of rail based movement was employed, with timber truckways laid down in 1724 (probably a crude guidance system) some 250 feet long. To serve the new steam technology, the construction of Keyham Yard (the southern part of North Yard) was commissioned in 1846 and completed in 1853. As this location was detached from the original site, a tunnel was included to connect the two. The required Act of Parliament received Royal Assent on 2 June 1854, and construction commenced in April 1855, completed in April 1857. It is 2,580 feet long, with five air shafts and one open section – it remains extant today for utility services. Originally it was only paved for pedestrians and light wagons, but had always been intended for railway use – though it was only 12 feet high.

It was to be 1860 before a proper railway was laid in the Dockyard. 6,750 feet of rails were purchased for the laying of a Broad Gauge line from the Boiler Shop to the South Basin in Keyham Steam Yard. More trackwork quickly followed in and around the main factory building, called the Quadrangle. Mention is made of a road traction engine, so either that, or horse/man power was used initially. More construction work was commissioned when W. Jackson was engaged to extend the size of North Basin. When he started the work the Admiralty bought him an Aveling & Porter locomotive (works No. 143 of 1865) and it is thought that this remained in use with the Admiralty afterwards.

Between the original Dockyard and the new Keyham Yard was the Gun Wharf. This establishment installed two gauges of tramway in 1867,

Broad Gauge turntable in South Yard 1992. Now at the Didcot Railway Centre.
PAUL BURKHALTER

The branch with dual gauge track. The barracks entrance bridge and the commodores house are in view. 1889.
TNA ADM 195/60

broad and 18 inch gauges, to move stores around the site and to the river wharf. Also in 1867 there were plans for connecting the tunnel with the Gun Wharf.

The Cornwall Railway was opened from Plymouth into Cornwall on 4 May 1859 and very soon the Admiralty was discussing the construction of a connecting line to the Dockyard. The agreement for this is dated 15 December 1865, with construction of a 5 furlong 9½ chain single broad gauge line descending 38½ feet at about 1 in 70 to the Dockyard from Keyham Junction. It was completed on 20 June 1867. Once the branch was open, the need for a railway through the tunnel became apparent. The Cornwall Railway were instructed to proceed with the purchase of materials in May 1875 'when at favourable prices' and implemented sometime between 1876-7. Due to the restricted size of the tunnel, only 12 feet high, a standard gauge railway was laid.

The L&SWR were advancing their railways westward and in May 1876 standard gauge trains reached Plymouth via Okehampton. As part of that work an additional rail was laid on the broad gauge GWR as far as Keyham junction, and on the branch to the Yard. The GWR provided a broad gauge 'shunting truck' specifically allocated for handling broad and standard gauge Dockyard traffic. The wagon was originally built by Hemmett in 1854 for the South Devon Railway as their No. 186. Taken into GWR stock as no. 10232 in June 1877 it was allocated for the Dockyard traffic in September 1878. The body was said to be 15ft long with 3ft wheels and a 9ft wheelbase. It was condemned in June 1886. Daily freight trains were worked into the Dockyard by both the GWR and L&SWR from their local depots in Plymouth.

Very early in Sir John Jacksons contract looking east. April 1896. TNA 195/61

At this time sailors were accommodated in old hulks moored in the river. This became increasingly unacceptable hence a land based barracks were built in the 1880s. This was constructed on land north of the Dockyard and adjacent to the branch railway. A siding was laid from the branch to bring materials for the Wardroom construction. In addition, a passenger platform was installed on the branch next to the barracks main entrance, which was used for the next 100 years for the movement of naval personnel between Devonport and other establishments.

The GWR broad gauge met its demise in May 1892, though the Dockyard branch still had the third rail in place in 1896.

As Naval vessels enlarged then the shore facilities needed to keep pace. At the close of the 19th century a vast undertaking was implemented at Devonport that would take nearly 10 years to construct and double to size of the Yard. Two wet basins and three dry docks covering 118 acres, they were known as Extension Works. Sir John Jackson was the contractor, and he utilised the most modern of construction methods including 25 miles of standard gauge temporary railways, with 25 steam engines, and an extensive wagon fleet. The railways were engaged with all aspects of the construction, from moving excavated material (where

Excavation for 4 dock. 2 Sept 1896. TNA 195/61

HL2599 of 1904. 25 May 1951.
DEVONPORT NAVAL HERITAGE CENTRE

some narrow gauge tramways were also laid), taking dredged shingle from barges to the concrete plants, mixed concrete, and material bought to the site from the main-line. Jackson had a large workshop/loco shed where maintenance and major repairs were undertaken. The contract was completed at the end of 1906 followed by an end-of-contract plant auction that included 18 locomotives, 536 wagons, two passenger coaches and 1,500 tons of rail.

In 1948 *No 1* (HL2399 of 1898) is carrying the Royal Crest at the North Yard loco shed.
PAUL BURKHALTER COLLECTION

No 2 (AB2221 of 1946) in North Yard. 1960s. C. HORSHAM

Also at the end of the 19th century, the Admiralty purchased more locomotives in readiness for the new enlarged Dockyard. Railways were installed by Jackson in the permanent works to run throughout the new facilities. In addition the elongated site (the barracks at the north, and docks and wharves extended southwards) resulted in the need to move the sailors and workforce in a speedy manner – and the Dockyard Train was implemented. By August 1897 a scheduled passenger service had commenced from the Barracks platform southwards. Once the Extension Works were finished in 1907 this service ran from one end of the Dockyard to the other on a regular 30 minutes basis, the jouney taking about 20 minutes. Two sets of 'carriages' were in use, though converted goods trucks would be a more accurate description, plus a flat wagon for any materials. In true Naval tradition, a strict class system was in use

The barracks platform with roof about 1966. PAUL BURKHALTER COLLECTION

based on rank – the workmen and ordinary sailors conveyed in closed goods wagons fitted with benches, then a total of six classes up to a single upholstered compartment for the Admiral Superintendent. The train conveyed the King and Queen on 8 March 1902 when at Devonport for the launch of the battleship *HMS Queen*, an event that was commemorated by the addition of the Royal Crest to the train locomotive *No. 1*.

Freight was the predominant user of the Dockyard Railway, with goods arriving from the mainline over the branch connection, and internal movement throughout the yard delivering goods to ships and refit materials to docks. An extensive fleet of internal user wagons was built up, usually from second-hand main-line wagons sometimes rebuilt in the Yard's workshops. Most had to be reduced in height to pass through the tunnel, those that were not had notices painted on the sides banning tunnel use, though sometimes mishaps occurred when these were ignored. In addition much use was made of rail-gauge cranes, many of which were equipped to shunt wagons. Occasional naval passenger special trains ran onto the Dockyard system from around the UK to deliver or collect naval personnel to their ships moored alongside.

The single line through the tunnel was controlled by a crude system of bell rings. A misunderstanding between the two ends resulted in a fatal accident on 7 July 1907 when a 15 year-old telegraph boy was killed when two trains were allowed in opposite directions, and collided head-on. The Admiralty was criticised at the Inquest, and thereafter quickly installed a standard Miniature Staff train control system. One of the locomotives involved, *No. 5*, was sufficiently damaged to be scrapped. The branch from the mainline at Keyham to the Dockyard has always been controlled by a single-line staff, possession of which is required by the driver of a train before proceeding.

More locomotives arrived, particularly during the Great War, then in the preparations for the Second World War one dock was enlarged. The contractor, Edmund Nuttall, Sons & Co, employed two Ruston &

Troop train on 5 wharf with Australian troops for embarkation aboard the troopship *HMAT Takada*. 18 July 1919.
PAUL BURKHALTER COLLECTION

No 18 with a freight train in North Yard 1950s.
PAUL BURKHALTER COLLECTION

Hornsby standard gauge diesel locomotives. At a similar time Bernard Sunley & Co. enlarged the water storage at the Yard and bought a selection of narrow gauge locos here.

It was to be 1955 before the wholly Admiralty steam locomotive fleet was changed to diesel. Ten new Planet type 0-4-0 diesel locomotives were obtained from FC Hibberd. The steam locos were phased out before 1966.

The passenger service ceased on Friday 13 May 1966 with much ceremony, and most of the Dockyard workforce turned out to ride or

The gateway between the barracks and the dockyard in September 2006.
PAUL BURKHALTER COLLECTION

A busy scene at the exchange sidings in the 1950s. On the left is *No.2*.
HUGH DAVIES/PHOTOS FROM THE FIFTIES

watch the final train. Loco *No. 2* was specially steamed to provide the motive power. The replacement bus service continues to this day. The freight service gradually declined as road transport became more effective, with the rail use of the tunnel ceasing on 10 November 1982. However new submarine docks built between 1975 and 1980 included new trackwork for the special loads arising from refitting nuclear submarines.

Two visits of the Royal Train to the Dockyard Railway have been ascertained. The Duke of Edinburgh attended the annual Armada Dinner in the wardroom of HMS Drake on 11 July 1967, and then returned to London by the Royal Train. The train had worked down the previous night, and was bought to Keyham after stabling at Millbay during the

One of the ex-Army Drewrys by the Rail Gate to the Barracks. 10 June 2004.
PAUL BURKHALTER

Steel reinforcement for construction work being delivered by rail. September 2000.
PAUL BURKHALTER

afternoon and evening. Hauled by Warship class locomotives the train was scheduled to depart the Barracks Platform at 22.50, the royal carriages being attached to the Paddington sleeper train in Plymouth Station. On 11 May 1970 the Duke of Edinburgh arrived on the Royal Train overnight from Slough after spending the night on the Heathfield branch. The train was scheduled to arrive at Keyham at 9.30 a.m. before reversing onto the Dockyard branch and stopping at 9.45. The train then returned empty immediately to Old Oak Common. The detailed operating instructions even note that the 'Barracks platform is 6 inches below standard height'.

A departure of the Commanding Officer of HMS Drake is recorded in the Drake Diaries, when on 23 February 1988 Commodore Kettlewell departed HMS Drake 'in a specially decorated dockyard train resplendent in new livery, bunting and name plate *Sir Francis Drake* 12.5, thus alluding to the 'express's' top speed!'

The Dockyard Railway was used in the film *Force Ten from Navarone* made in 1978. Actors Robert Shaw, Harrison Ford and Edward Fox used the area around the South Smithery as a wartime location depicting a port in Yugoslavia under German control. One of the Planet locos, driven by Clifford Whitrow, and a rake of BR and Dockyard trucks played a large part in the scenes shot at night.

InterCity power car 43181 was named *Devonport Royal Dockyard 1693-1993* at a ceremony at Plymouth Station on Thursday 25 November 1993. At 9.15 a.m. on Platform 4, Flag Officer Plymouth, Vice-Admiral Sir Roy Newman KCB, unveiled the nameplate to a fanfare of Marine trumpeters.

GBRf class 66 locomotive 66775 worked into the Dockyard branch to Drake Platform to be named *HMS Argyll* on 11 July 2017. COLIN J. MARSDEN

The branch line was relayed in 1992 by contractor Grant Lyon Eagre, who utilised their Trackmobile shunter on site. Replacement locomotives for the Planet types were necessary so two ex-Army Drewry diesels arrived in March 1993.

The Dockyard was privatised in April 1987 and the railway came under the control of the company running the Yard, Devonport Management Ltd, on 4 October 1993. The new company wished to diversify from Naval work so took on a number of railway contracts that saw locomotives and carriages on site for a variety of work. Many of these items arrived via the branch connection, whilst others came by road.

In 1993 Devonport Dockyard was selected to provide the refitting facilities for the 16,000 tonne Vanguard class of nuclear submarines. No. 9 dock in North Yard was converted for this work between 1999 and 2002 and a new railway constructed to connect with a new waste storage building constructed at the north of 5 basin and No. 14 dock. This

EWS 66081 the first of this class to visit the Dockyard alongside a dockyard Drewry. 22 Jun 2000. PAUL BURKHALTER

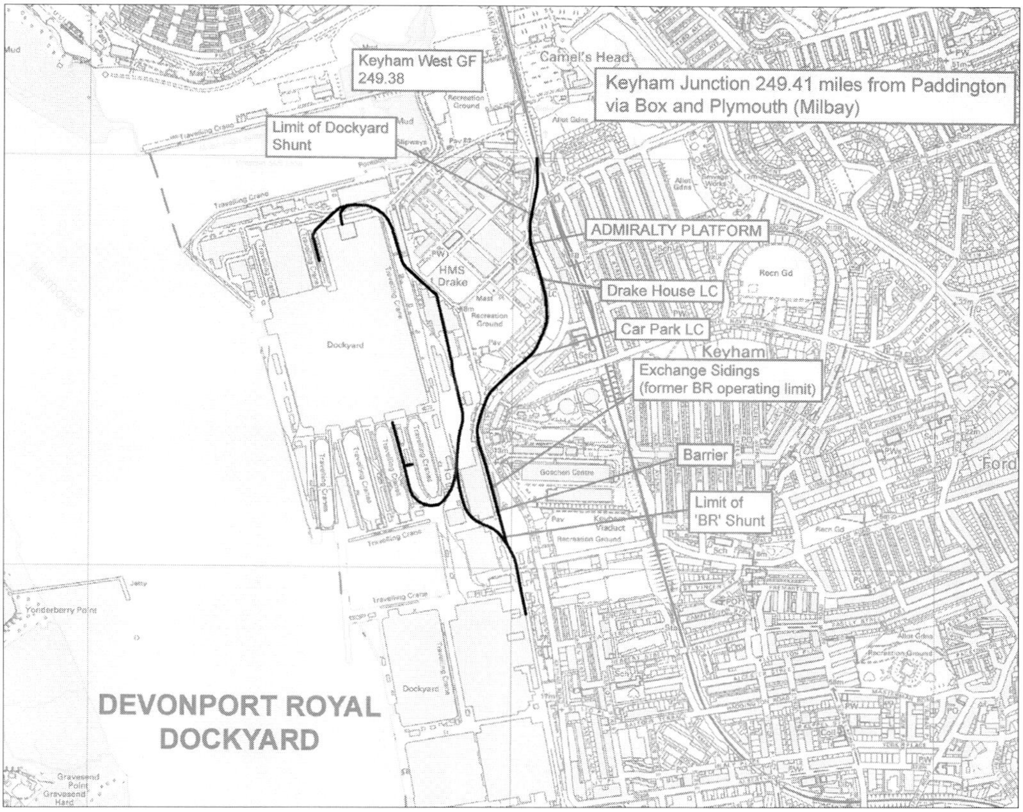

Plan showing the current layout in 2017 highlighted.

1,500m long standard gauge railway was built under contract by Edmund Nuttall Ltd. The track is set in a concrete strip, and also includes three wagon turntables, six turnouts and one crossover. The first of the new rails were laid in March 2001. Clayton especially manufactured two new diesel shunting locomotives, and two new specialist flat-bed wagons were provided. All existing railways to the north of the North Dock Pumping Station were replaced by this new system, partially laid on a new alignment. The last usage of the old track was in August 2000, and the first test runs on the new track commenced on 23 August 2001, with full use the following month.

In 2008, the branch again received attention when Babcock Rail used some on-track plant and the tamper *William Arrol* to relay track.

Full details of the extensive fleet of locomotives was included in this author's book *Devonport Dockyard Railway* (Twelveheads Press, 1996) so only a tabular record is appended. The most recent are two Clayton built diesel locomotives delivered in 2000 specifically designed for movements in connection with the refitting of nuclear submarines, the only use that the Dockyard makes of the railway.

Admiralty / Ministry of Defence
Gauge : 4ft 8 ½ins

1	2	3	4	5	6	7	8	9
-	-	4wTG	OC	AP	143	1865	New	-
	-	0-4-0ST	OC	JF	7710	1897	New	s/s
5	-	0-4-0ST	OC	FE		1884	(a) ?)	(2)
1	-	0-4-0ST	OC	HL	2399	1898	New	Scr 1948
2	-	0-4-0ST	OC	HL	2400	1898	New	Scr
3	MIDDLESBROUGH	0-4-0ST	OC	B+	296	1882	-	-
		reb Sir J.Jackson, Keyham				1903	(b)	(3)
4	-	0-4-0ST	OC	HLT	340	1880	(b) ?	s/s
6	-	0-4-0T*	OC	HL	2599	1904	New	Scr 1955
7	-	0-4-0ST	OC	HL	2820	1910	New	Scr 1957
8	-	0-4-0ST	OC	HL	2821	1910	New	Scr c1955
9	-	0-4-0ST	OC	AB	1406	1915	(c)	Scr 1957
10	-	0-4-0ST	OC	AB	1379	1914	New	Scr 8/1956
11	-	0-4-0ST	OC	AB	1380	1914	New	Scr 1957
12	-	0-4-0ST	OC	AE	1690	1915	New	(4)
13	-	0-4-0ST	OC	AB	1397	1915	New	(5)
14	-	0-4-0ST	OC	HL	3200	1916	New	Scr 1957
15	-	0-4-0ST	OC	HL	3201	1916	New	Scr 1957
16	-	0-4-0ST	OC	AB	1516	1919	New	Scr 11/1955
17	-	0-4-0ST	OC	AB	2071	1939	New	(7)
18	-	0-4-0ST	OC	AB	2137	1942	New	(8)
(19) 2	-	0-4-0ST	OC	AB	2221	1946	New	(6)
19	-	0-4-0ST	OC	WB	2962	1950	New	(9)
YARD No.4856		4w	DM	FH	3737	1955	New (d)	(12)
YARD No.4857		4w	DM	FH	3741	1955	New	Scr 1977
YARD No.4858 ++		4w	DM	FH	3744	1955	New	(16)
YARD No.4859 ++		4w	DM	FH	3746	1955	New	(11)
YARD No.4860 ++ $		4w	DM	FH	3747	1955	New	(14)
YARD No.5197		4w	DM	FH	3773	1955	New	Scr 1980
YARD No.5198 $		4w	DM	FH	3774	1955	New	(15)
YARD No.5199 ++		4w	DM	FH	3775	1955	New	(15)
YARD No.5200		4w	DM	FH	3776	1956	New	(13)
YARD No.5332 ++		4w	DM	FH	3816	1956	New	(12)
-	-	4w	DH	S&H	7503	1967	New	(10)
249 / YARD No.10433		0-4-0	DM	-	VF	5258	1945	- -
-	-	-	-	DC	2177	1945	(e)	(17)
230 / YARD No.10432		0-4-0	DM	VF	5265	1945	-	-
-	-	-	-	DC	2184	1945	(f)	(17)

\+ Works plates read 'Lennox Lange & Co., 1883'.

++ Locos which are known to be/have been allocated to the South Yard.
* converted from a crane tank.
$ locos FH 3747 and 3774 appear to have exchanged identities at some date.

(a) loco delivered new to Admiralty, location unspecified; possibly No.5 here.
(b) ex Sir J.Jackson, Devonport Dockyard contract, 1/2/1907.
(c) ex Admiralty, Rosyth, Fife.
(d) to RNAD, Ernesettle, c7/1960; returned c1960.
(e) ex Long Marston Depot, Warwickshire, after overhaul by YEC, 4/3/1993.
(f) ex Long Marston Depot, Warwickshire, after overhaul by YEC, 5/3/1993.

(2) damaged beyond repair in a collison with No.3 (B 296) on 6/7/1907; scrapped.
(3) to Wm. Gray & Co Ltd, West Hartlepool, Co.Durham, c1935 (after 10/1935).
(4) adapted as a stationary boiler, 1957; scrapped c1959.
(5) scrapped 1959 (after 1/1959).
(6) purchased by Hudsons of Dudley Ltd; to Small & Lewis, Gloucester; thence to Dowty Railway Preservation Society, Ashchurch, Gloucestershire, 3/1968. Now at Dean Forest Railway in a dismantled state.
(7) purchased by Hudsons of Dudley Ltd; to Small & Lewis, Gloucester, for scrap, 3/1968.
(8) purchased by Hudsons of Dudley Ltd; to Small & Lewis, Gloucester, 3/1968; scrapped by Avon Metals Ltd, Cheltenham, Gloucestershire, 3/1968.
(9) to Great Western Society, Bodmin, Cornwall, 26/2/1969.
(10) to Portsmouth Dockyard, Hampshire, 3/3/1969
(11) to George Cohen, Sons & Co Ltd, 3/12/1970: thence to Wagon Repairs Ltd, Stoke-on-Trent, Staffordshire, 1/1971.
(12) to George Cohen, Sons & Co Ltd, 3/12/1970: to Wagon Repairs Ltd, Gloucester, 1970.
(13) to Cornwall Railway Museum, Zelah, Cornwall, 6/4/1983.
(14) to NATO Mooring & Support Depot, Fairlie, Strathclyde, 8/1984.
(15) to scrapyard, Farrington Gurney, Avon, 7/10/1993; dismantled there and components to Festionog Railway, Portmadoc, Merioneth.
(16) to J. Wells & Son, Porchester, Hampshire, for scrap, 3/12/1993.
(17) to Devonport Royal Dockyard Ltd, with site, 13/3/1997.

Devonport Royal Dockyard Ltd / Babcock International Group
Gauge : 4ft 8½ins

1	2	3	4	5	6	7	8	9
249	YARD No.10433	0-4-0	DM	VF	5258	1945	-	-
-	-	-		DC	2177	1945	(a)	(1)
230	YARD No.10432	0-4-0	DM	VF	5265	1945	-	-
-	-	-	-	DC	2184	1945	(a)	(2)
RTU 1	DENNIS	4w	DM	CE	B4314A	2000	New	-
RTU 2	HENRY	4w	DM	CE	B4314B	2000	New	(3)

(a) ex Ministry of Defence, with site, 13/3/1997.

(1) to John Payne, Long Marston, Warwickshire, 10/2/2004.
(2) to Andrew Briddon, Elsecar Steam Railway, South Yorkshire, 6/12/2005.
(3) to Clayton 30/3/2016 for major rebuild. To Wirksworth for trials 11/5/2016, returned to Devonport 19/5/2016

B Sunley & Co Ltd
Contract for work at 'Admiralty Reservoir, Devonport', 1939 -
Gauge : 2ft 0in ?

1	2	3	4	5	6	7	8	9
-	-	4w	BE	WR	1395	1939	New	s/s
-	-	4w	BE	WR	1396	1939	New	s/s
-	-	4w	BE	WR	1397	1939	New	s/s
-	-	4w	DM	R&R	88	1939	New	(1)
-	-	4w	DM	R&R	95	1939	New	(1)

(1) this company advertised four such locos for sale from London on 1/11/1944; s/s.

William Jackson
Devonport Contract

Construction, by this London based contractor, of an extension to the North (No.3) Basin at Devonport Dockyard for the Admiralty, 1865 – 1867.

Gauge : 4ft 8 ½ins

-	-	4wTG	OC	AP	143	1865	New	(1)

(1) possibly to Admiralty Devonport.

Edmund Nuttall, Sons & Co (London) Ltd
Devonport Contract

Contract for the enlargement of No.10 Dock at Devonport Dockyard for the Admiralty, from 5/1937 until 5/1940. The locomotives were used to move wet concrete from the central mixing plant to the working site.

Gauge : 4ft 8 ½ins

-	-	4w	DM	RH	186314	1937	New	(1)
-	-	4w	DM	RH	186316	1937	New	(2)

(1) to Colnbrook Plant Depot, Buckinghamshire, by 5/1940; s/s.

(2) to Glascoed (ROF) contract, Gwent, by 9/1939.

Sir John Jackson Ltd

Sir John Jackson until 1898

Devonport Dockyard Contract

Construction of major extensions at Devonport Dockyard, Keyham for the Admiralty. The work was to occupy 118 acres, doubling the size of the dockyard, and included two wet basins and three dry docks. Jackson's tender was accepted on 1/1/1896 and the contract was let on 13/10/1896. Work had started by 3/1896 and lasted until 1907. 25 miles of temporary railways were used, with workshop facilities and a locomotive shed for 18 engines. Eleven locomotives were present in 7/1896, fourteen (four six-wheeled the rest four-wheeled) in 7/1899, and 25 were used in total.

Gauge : 4ft 8 ½ins

1	2	3	4	5	6	7	8	9
-	-	0-4-0ST	OC	HL	2329	1896	New	s/s
-	HAMOAZE	0-4-0ST	OC	B	229	1876	(a)	(1)

1	2	3	4	5	6	7	8	9
-	MIDDLESBROUGH	0-4-0ST	OC	B	+ 296	1882	-	-
	-	-	-	reb	-	1903	(b)	(2)
-	GLASGOW	0-4-0ST	OC	AB	185	1877	(c)	(3)
	-	0-4-0ST	OC	HC	293	1887	(d)	s/s
-	KEYHAM	0-6-0T	IC	HC	318	1889	(d)	(4)
-	NOTTINGHAM	0-6-0ST	IC	HE	1	1865	(d)	(5)
-	TAMAR	0-4-0ST	OC	HE	360	1884	(d)	(6)
-	DEVONPORT	0-6-0T	IC	HE	401	1886	(d)	(7)
-	-	0-6-0ST	IC	HE	437	1888	(d)	(8)
-	CLYDE	0-4-0ST	OC	MW	714	1879	(d)	(9)
-	DEVONPORT	0-6-0ST	IC	MW	951	1885	(d)	(10)
-	TORCROSS	0-4-0ST	OC	MW	1036	1887	(d)	(11)
-	LORD NELSON	0-4-0ST	OC	MW	1090	1888	(d)	(12)
148	WESTMINSTER	0-6-0T	IC	SS	3474	1888	(d)	(13)
-	DON JOSE	0-4-0ST	OC	AB	810	1897	New	(14)
-	TYNE	0-4-0ST	OC	MW	1051	1888	(e)	(15)
-	LORD ROBERTS	0-4-0ST	OC	MW	1018	1887	(f)	s/s
-	MOUNT EDGCUMBE	0-4-0ST	OC	MW	1342	1897	(f)	s/s
174	BURNTISLAND	0-4-0ST	OC	AB	797	1897	(g)	(16)
-	MAGGIE	0-4-0ST	OC	HC	287	1887	(h)	(17)
-	ETHEL	0-4-0ST	OC	AB	853	1900	New	(15)
-	KATHLEEN	0-4-0ST	OC	AB	867	1900	New	s/s
-	VICTORIA	0-4-0ST	OC	AB	887	1900	New	(18)
-	DOVER	0-4-0ST	OC	AB	891	1901	New	(19)

\+ Works plates read "Lennox Lange & Co., 1883".

(a) origins unknown.

(b) possibly ex Middlesbrough Dock (1882-1889) contract, Co.Durham; here by 2/1897.

(c) earlier at North Sunderland Harbour (1886-1889) contract, Northumberland.

(d) ex/earlier T.A. Walker, Manchester Ship Canal contract, Lancashire (earlier names were – HC 293, FLIXTON; HC 318, HEATON; HE 1, SWANSEA; HE 360, LYTHAM; HE 401, GLOUCESTER; HE 437, MANCHESTER; MW 714, MARTIN; MW 951, ACCRINGTON; MW 1036, BARHAM; MW 1090, CADISHEAD; SS 3474, OPENSHAW.)

(e) earlier T.A. Walker, Manchester Ship Canal contract, Lancashire, CANTERBURY; possibly then at Jacksons' Tynemouth Pier contract, Northumberland.

(f) ex Pauling & Co Ltd, Westbury (GWR) contract, Wiltshire, probably 4/1900.

(g) ex Burntisland Harbour contract, Fife.

(h) ex P , 27/1/1900; earlier Electro-Chemical Co Ltd, St Helens, Lancashire; originally William P. Hartley, Aintree, Liverpool.

(1) sold here (for £225, so possibly for scrap), 30/1/1907; s/s

(2) to H.M. Dockyard, Devonport, 3, 1/2/1907.

(3) to War Dept, Heytesbury Military Railway, Wiltshire, by 2/1916; but later for sale by Sir John Jackson Ltd, 8/1921; s/s.

(4) later John Griffith & Sons Ltd, Glenburn Colliery, Skelmersdale, Lancashire.

(5) later Samuel Williams & Sons Ltd, Dagenham Dock, Essex, No.6, after 1909.

(6) to Ferrol Dockyard contract, Spain, after 1/1906,by 6/1910; later with H. Covington & Sons, Battersea, London, by 1923.

(7) for sale here, 31/1/1907; not sold and to Grays Plant Depot, Essex; later Amesbury Camp (War Dept) contract, Wiltshire.

(8) for sale here, 31/1/1907; but later at Grays Plant Depot, Essex, 1921; s/s.

(9) sold here (for £91, so possibly for scrap), 30/1/1907; s/s

(10) for sale here, 31/1/1907; but later Grays Plant Depot, Essex, DEVONPORT, for sale, 8/1921; to Samuel Williams & Sons Ltd, Dagenham Dock, Essex.

(11) to Cochran & Co (Annan) Ltd, Annan, Dumfries-shire, after 31/1/1907.

(12) sold from here, 31/1/1907; disposal unknown.

(13) later Grays Plant Depot, Essex; to Thos W. Ward Ltd, with site, 1924; s/s after 8/1935.

(14) for sale here, 5/2/1907; s/s

(15) for sale here, 31/1/1907; s/s

(16) later Singapore Harbour contract; then to Vancouver Harbour contract, Canada 1913; later used on Upper Nile Barrage contract, Egypt, by 2/1929; s/s.

(17) to Ferrol Dockyard contract, Spain, 1910; later with S. Pearson & Son Ltd, Gretna (MoM) contract, Dumfries-shire, 1916; thence to Gas Light & Coke Co, Beckton, London, No.37, by 1919.

(18) later at Grays Plant Depot, Essex; to Thos.W. Ward Ltd, with site, 1924: thence to Thos.W. Ward Ltd, Inverkeithing Yard, Fife, JJ 711, after 1926, by 1935.

(19) later at Grays Plant Depot, Essex; to Thos.W. Ward Ltd, with site, 1924: thence to John Spencer Ltd, Newburn Steelworks, Newcastle-upon-Tyne, 1932.

Grant Lyon Eagre Ltd (standard gauge)
Contract to relay the branch in 1992

1	2	3	4	5	6	7	8	9
-	-	4w	DM	S&H	7510	1967	03/1992	by12/1992

Rail cranes

Sir John Jackson, Keyham Dock, Devonport
Gauge 7ft 0in / 4ft 8½in (Steam Navvy's)

1	2	3	4	5	6	7	8	9
-	-	4w	VB/5t	JB	997	1896	new	-
-	-	4w	VB/5t	JB	998	1896	new	-
-	-	4w	VB/7t	JB	1047A	1896	new	-
-	-	4w	VB/7t	JB	1047B	1896	new	-
-	-	4w	VB/5t	JB	1074A	1897	new	-
-	-	4w	VB/5t	JB	1074B	1897	new	-
-	-	4w	VB/5t	JB	1074C	1897	new	-
-	-	4w	VB/5t	JB	1074D	1897	new	-

Gauge : 4ft 8½ins (Cranes)

1	2	3	4	5	6	7	8	9
-	-	4w	VB/5t	TS	4982	1895	new	-
-	-	4w	VB/5t	TS	4983	1895	new	-
-	-	4w	VB/5t	TS	4984	1895	new	-
-	-	4w	VB/5t	TS	5074	1896	new	-
-	-	4w	VB/5t	TS	5122	1896	new	-
-	-	4w	VB/5t	TS	5172	1896	new	-
-	-	4w	VB/5t	JB	978A	1896	new	-
-	-	4w	VB/5t	JB	978B	1896	new	-
-	-	4w	VB/5t	JB	978C	1896	new	-
-	-	4w	VB/5t	JB	978D	1896	new	-
-	-	4w	VB/5t	JB	978E	1896	new	-
-	-	4w	VB/5t	TS	5225	1897	new	-
-	-	4w	VB/5t	TS	5226	1897	new	-
-	-	4w	VB/5t	TS	5500	1898	new	-
-	-	4w	VB/5t	TS	5501	1898	new	-
-	-	4w	VB/5t	TS	5502	1898	new	-
-	-	4w	VB/5t	TS	5503	1898	new	-
-	-	4w	VB/5t	TS	5504	1898	new	-
-	-	4w	VB/5t	TS	5505	1898	new	-

Admiralty / MOD - Navy Dept, Devonport, Plymouth
Gauge : 4ft 8½ins

-	-	4w	VB/5t	G	178	1890	new	-
-	-	4w	VB/7t	G	253	1892	new	-
-	-	4w	VB/5t	G	391	1896	new	(1)
-	-	4w	VB/5t	G	479	1897	new	-
-	-	4w	VB/5t	G	631	1900	new	-
-	-	4w	VB/7t	G	849	1903	new	-
-	-	4w	VB/10t	G	854	1903	new	-
-	-	4w	VB/10t	G	855	1903	new	-
-	-	4w	VB/10t	G	885	1903	new	-
-	-	4w	VB/7t	HJC	421	1906	new	-
-	-	4w	VB/7t	HJC	422	1906	new	-
-	-	4w	VB/10t	G	1178	1909	new	-
-	-	4w	VB/10t	G	1179	1909	new	-
-	-	4w	VB/10t	G	1180	1909	new	-
-	-	4w	VB/10t	G	1181	1909	new	-
-	-	4w	VB/3t	JB	2345A	1910	new	-
-	-	4w	VB/3t	JB	2345B	1910	new	-
-	-	4w	VB/10t	JB	2813A	1914	new	-
-	-	4w	VB/10t	JB	2813B	1914	new	-

1	2	3	4	5	6	7	8	9
-	-	4w	VB/7t	G	1614	1915	new	-
-	-	4w	VB/7t	G	1615	1915	new	-
-	-	4w	VB/7t	G	1646	1915	new	(2)
-	-	4w	VB/7t	G	1647	1915	new	(3)
-	-	4w	VB/7t	G	1648	1915	new	-
-	-	4w	VB/7t	G	1649	1915	new	-
-	-	4w	VB/1½t	TS	8822	1916	new	-
-	-	4w	VB/1½t	TS	8823	1916	new	-
-	-	4w	VB/1½t	S&P	B4107	1916	new	-
-	-	4w	VB/1½t	S&P	B4108	1916	new	-
-	-	4w	VB/10t	G	1808	1918	new	-
-	-	4w	VB/10t	G	1809	1918	new	-
-	-	4w	VB/5t	TS	11640	1931	new	-
-	-	4w	VB/3t	TS	12968	1939	new	-
YARD No.173		4w	VB/5t	T&H	1431	1940	new	-
YARD No.176		4w	VB/10t	G	2554	1940	new	Scr 28/2/1976
YARD No.175		4w	VB/10t	G	2555	1940	new	-
YARD No.174		4w	VB/10t	G	2561	1940	new	Scr 8/1973
YARD No.186		4w	VB/3t	TS	13639	1940	new	-
YARD No.270		4w	VB/7t	G	2597	1942	new	-
YARD No.258		4w	VB/5t	T&H	1520	1943	new	-
YARD No.259		4w	VB/5t	T&H	1521	1943	new	-
YARD No.331		4w	VB/10t	G	2677	1943	new	Scr 1967
YARD No.332		4w	VB/10t	G	2678	1943	new	-
YARD No.353		4w	VB/10t	G	2810	1946	new	-
YARD No.354		-	Steam	Coles	-	-	-	-
YARD No.370		4w	VB/10t	G	2822	1947	new	-
YARD No.388		4w	VB/10t	G	2826	1948	new	-
YARD No.411		4w	VB/10t	G	2841	1950	new	-
YARD No.410		4w	VB/10t	G	2842	1950	new	-
YARD No.412		-	Steam	-	-	-	-	-
YARD No.429		4w	VB/10t	G	2853	1950	new	-
YARD No.428		4w	VB/10t	G	2854	1950	new	-
-	-	4w	VB/10t	G	2882	1950	new	-
-	-	4w	VB/10t	G	2883	1950	new	-
YARD No.444		4w	VB/10t	G	2887	1952	new	-
YARD No.447		4w	DE/5t	TS	19393	1952	new	-
YARD No.448		4w	DE/5t	TS	19394	1952	new	-
YARD No.4896		4w	D/3t	TS	23507	1956	new	cr 12/1967
YARD No.4897		4w	D/3t	TS	23508	1956	new	-
YARD No.4898		4w	D/3t	TS	23509	1956	new	-
YARD No.4899		4w	D/3t	TS	23510	1956	new	-

1	2	3	4	5	6	7	8	9
YARD No.4900		4w	D/3t	TS	23511	1956	new	-
YARD No.4901		4w	D/3t	TS	23512	1956	new	-
YARD No.4902		4w	D/6t	TS	23513	1956	new	-
YARD No.4903		4w	D/6t	TS	23514	1956	new	-
YARD No.4904		4w	D/6t	TS	23515	1956	new	-
YARD No.4905		4w	D/6t	TS	23516	1956	new	-
YARD No.4906		4w	D/6t	TS	23517	1956	new	-
YARD No.5184		4w	D3t	TS	23806	1956	new	-
YARD No.5185		4w	D/3t	TS	23807	1956	new	-
YARD No.5186		4w	D/3t	TS	23808	1956	new	-
YARD No.5187		4w	D/3t	TS	23809	1956	new	-
YARD No.5188		4w	D/3t	TS	23810	1956	new	rebuilt as 6t 11/1967
YARD No.5189		4w	D/3t	TS	23811	1956	new	-
YARD No.5190		4w	D/6t	TS	23812	1956	new	(4)
YARD No.5191		4w	D/6t	TS	23813	1956	new	-
YARD No.5192		4w	D/6t	TS	23814	1956	new	-
YARD No.5193		4w	D/6t	TS	23812	1956	new	(4)
YARD No.5194		4w	D/6t	TS	23816	1956	new	-
-		4w	D/10t	TS	24528	1958	new	-
YARD No.7695		4w	D/6t	TS	25269	1961	new	-
YARD No.7696		4w	D/6t	TS	25270	1961	new	-
YARD No.9103		4w	DE/10t	TS	26459	1967	new	s/s c1990
YARD No.9282		4w	D/10t	TS		1968	new	-

to Llanelly Construction Co. 1936
to Plymouth & Devonport Ship Breaking
to Borough of Plymouth
to Plym Valley Railway 1985

SOURCES AND ACKNOWLEDGEMENTS

The original research for this section was undertaken in the early 1990s and resulted in the publication of my book *Devonport Dockyard Railway* in 1996. In addition to the acknowledgements contained in the original book, the following have provided further help: Alex Betteny, Peter Briddon, Paul Santillo, Russell Wear; Robin Weywell. Mary Wills,

FUTHER READING

Brimacombe, P. *The History of HMS Drake* for HMS Drake by Mor Marketing 1998

Burkhalter, P. *Devonport Dockyard Railway* Twelveheads Press 1996

Burns, Lt. Cdr. K. V., *The Devonport Dockyard Story* Maritime Books 1984

Coad, J.G. *The Royal Dockyards 1690-1850* Scolar Press for RCHME 1989

Efford Fort. The narrow gauge tramway. 29 September 1961.
© PLYMOUTH CITY COUNCIL (ARTS & HERITAGE) CITY ENGINEERS COLLECTION

Efford Fort

One of the ring of defensive works for Plymouth constructed between 1865 and 1869 described in the section on Crownhill Fort. In later years these structures have been utilised for many purposes, and in the Second World War the barrack casements were used to store ammunition. For this purpose an 18 inch gauge tramway was laid to connect the casements to the south of the central area. The Ministry of Defence gave up the fort in 1961, and it is now occupied by others. Some of the track survives.

Source

Pye. A, and Woodward. F, *The Historic Defences of Plymouth,* Cornwall County Council 1996

Efford Fort. Note the plate turntable lower left. 29 September 1961.
© PLYMOUTH CITY COUNCIL (ARTS & HERITAGE)

RAF Mountbatten

During the Great War the usefulness of air warfare was quickly appreciated. Aircraft were in their infancy and seaplanes were seen as useful in sea defence and attack. Plymouth was selected as a base, and land on the Mountbatten peninsula acquired for a Royal Naval Air Station (RNAS). Initially named RNAS Cattewater, it was opened in April 1917 and became operational in August of the same year. Construction was said to be by the Aircraft Construction Company, who used narrow gauge tramways to move the excavated soil from the hanger areas. Once the site was operational (and a change of name to RAF Cattewater in April 1918) the existing Mountbatten breakwater (completed in 1881) was used to launch and land the Short 184 seaplanes. This was facilitated by the use of an ex-Dockyard steam rail mounted crane on standard gauge track laid

The crane track extended from the Mountbatten Breakwater to the hangers.
PAUL BURKHALTER COLLECTION

The breakwater and ex-dockyard crane to hoist ashore Short 184 seaplanes.
PLYMOUTH LIBRARIES P000087639

direct on the surface of the breakwater. The track ran off the breakwater and in front of the hangers. The end of this use is not recorded, but the base was run-down after the end of the war in 1918, until revived in 1925 when there is no evidence of the rails or crane.

SOURCES
PWDRO: PCC/76/5/5474
Clamp, A. *The story of Mountbatten* 1980
Wasley, G. *RAF Mountbatten* Halsgrove 2006

Royal William Yard

The Royal Navy had possessed a base in Plymouth from the late 17th century onwards and this required a supply system for the fleet stationed here. By the early 19th century the storehouses were scattered around the waterfront and were not very efficient. In suitable grand fashion the Victualling Board of the Admiralty decided in November 1822 to construct a new Yard 'capable of embracing every requisite object' by way of naval supplies, and some 19 acres of land on the Stonehouse peninsula was purchased. Sir John Rennie (1794-1874) was appointed engineer and architect. Rennie was the son of the engineer who had started the construction of the great breakwater across the entrance to Plymouth Sound, and he had been carrying on this work after his father's death in 1821. The Victualling Yard was finally completed in 1834 and has been described as among the finest nineteenth century naval architecture in Britain. The whole Yard includes a one acre basin, its own extensive river wharfage, and buildings specifically designed as bakeries, slaughterhouses, dry stores and other buildings.

Aerial view of the Yard in the 1960s from the south.
DEVONPORT NAVAL HERITAGE CENTRE DAMAGED IMAGE RESTORED BY PAUL BURKHALTER

Up until 1891 the Navy had been supplied with ordnance by the War Department. With effect from 1 April in that year the Admiralty began to provide its own supplies and the Naval Ordnance Stores Department was formed to which a third of Royal William Yard was turned over in November 1891. A wall or fence was erected to divide the west end from the reminder of the ordinary stores area and it so existed for many years as a separate entity. For the movement of the heavy weights of armament an 18 inch gauge tramway was soon installed running from behind the

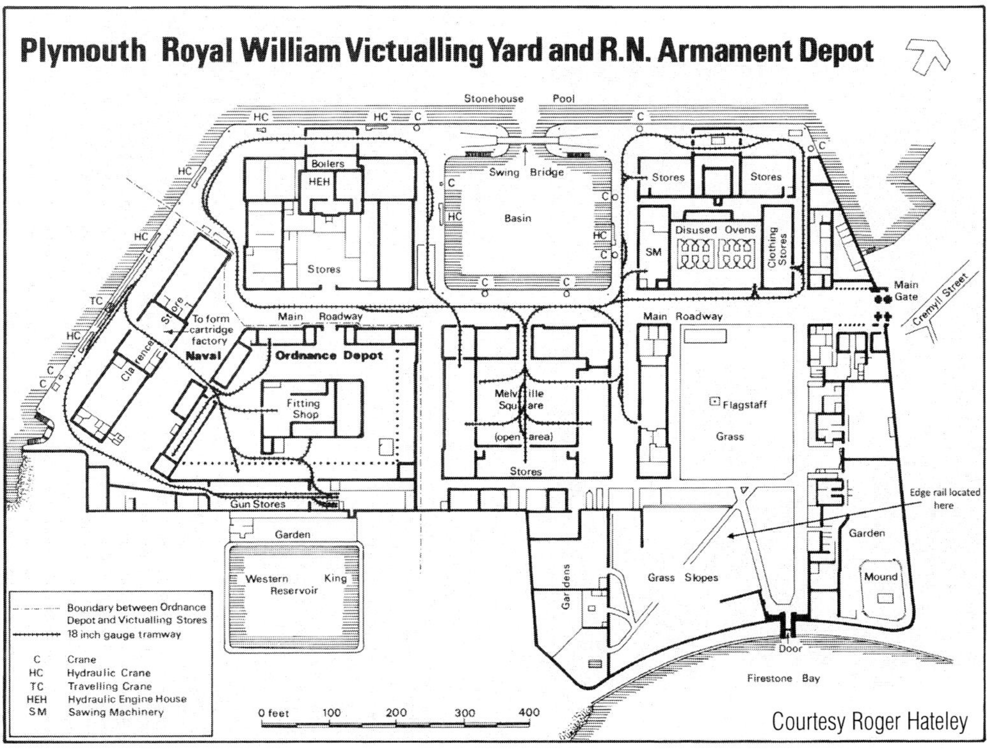

Courtesy Roger Hateley

July 1947 in the Ordnance Depot area at the rear of Clarence Block.
DEVONPORT NAVAL HERITAGE CENTRE N01314

Clarence Block to the wharf at the western end of the site, where there was a run-round loop. No exact date is recorded but it was in place by 1898. Nearly 500 yards of tramway had been laid by 1904 serving the various buildings, and two years later a store for 250lb spherical mines required yet more tramway, the length of track totalling 765 yards in the Naval Ordnance Depot alone. This extent remained through 1923.

For the Victualling Yard proper the length of its separate tramway system reached 1,450 yards in 1911. Surprisingly the two were not connected in any way, despite being so close together and of the same gauge.

The reign of the rail was not to last for long and before the Second World War most of the tramway had been replaced by concrete roadways for petrol powered trucks. Some rails did survive for the movement of heavy loads between the fitting shops in the cooperage and the old mine store, but had ceased to be employed by the middle of the 1960s.

The tramway was laid with 35lb/yd rail, flat bottomed dock-rail section on concrete, with blue brick paving in a strip between and to either side of the rail. Inventories of 1904 and 1911 reveal that there were four wagons for 2 ton payload in the Ordnance Depot, increasing in the latter year by a further eight for mines and sinkers. No similar details have survived for the Victualling Stores. There is no evidence of locomotive haulage, nor has any locomotive been noted for delivery here in extant manufacturers' records.

The Royal William Yard was never connected to the main-line despite the proximity of the Millbay Docks of the GWR (opened in 1850) and the L&SWR Stonehouse Pool Branch (opened in 1877), however during the annual visit of the Lords of the Admiralty in June 1892 the matter was raised of 'the desirability of a connection to the GWR' but nothing came of it.

Archaeological excavations undertaken for the development of the Yard, subsequent to the Ministry of Defence disposing of the site in the early 1990s, revealed one plate rail on stone sleeper blocks located in the

Inside an Ordnance workshop in July 1947.
DEVONPORT NAVAL HERITAGE CENTRE

Clarence Wharf narrow gauge tracks alongside a travelling crane.
PAUL BURKHALTER COLLECTION

Walled Garden. The other rail was not present so gauge was not determined. It is hypothesised that this was from the original construction of the site, though for what purpose is not known, nor the extent of the route.

SOURCES:

John Lyle-Carter of the (now defunct) Plymouth Development Corporation

Jonathan Coad

Devonport Naval Heritage Centre, uncatalogued records

Hampshire Record Office for the 1904, 1911 & 1923 inventories.

Plymouth City Museum for access to the Archeological Report.

Turnchapel Wharves

Shipbuilding had been carried out on this site since the early 19th century. It appears that it passed to the Bulteel family, in the form of the Turnchapel Wharves Company Ltd, in the 1880s.

Plans for improvements in the middle of 1884 show that a connection to the L&SWR Turnchapel Branch was proposed from the inception of the railway in 1883, and that the early limited river front facilities were being developed to take advantage of this. The Turnchapel line construction proceeded slowly, with the bridge over the Laira completed in 1887, but the whole line to Turnchapel was not opened until 5 September 1892. The connection with the branch was the subject of a private siding agreement dated 15 March 1896, between Thomas Bulteel and the L&SWR. Inter alia: 'L&SWR engines will do the shunting but if not available Thomas

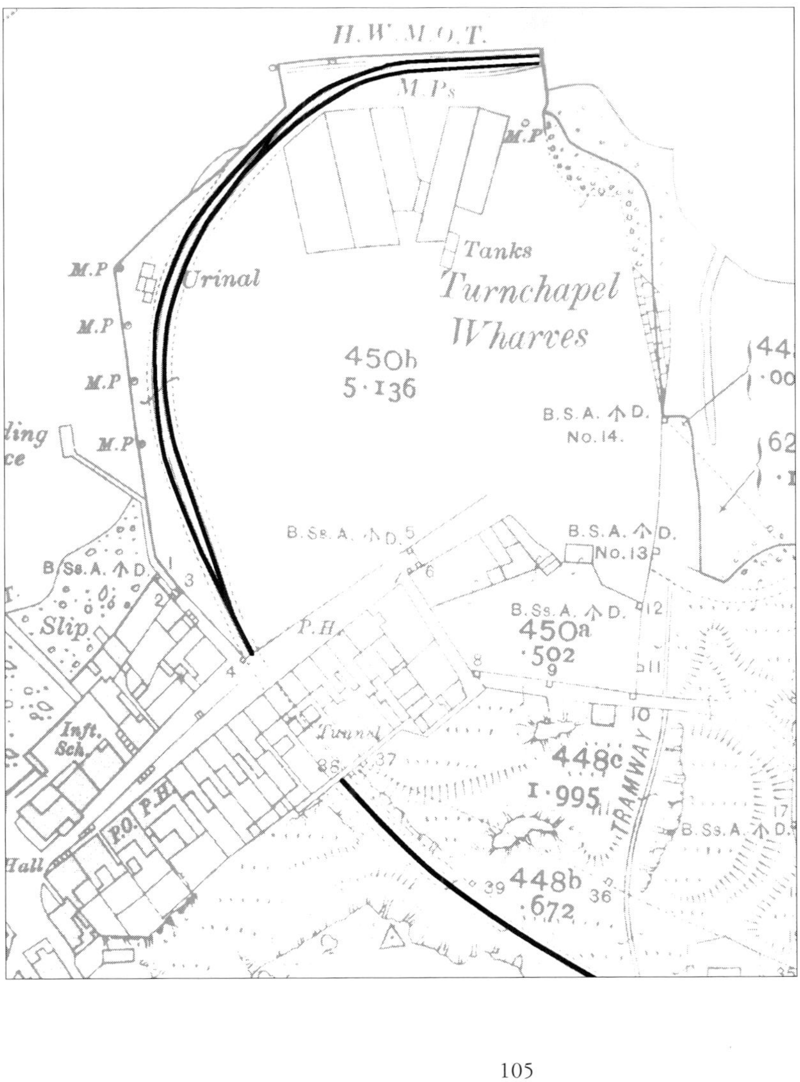

Turnchapel Tunnel in 1961. BERNARD MILLS

Bulteel will do the shunting by horse or other power'. To reach the Wharves, the line tunnelled under a road and some existing properties. A gate closed off the tunnel on the L&SWR side. Once onto the Wharves site the single line split into two which curved at a 200ft radius to the quay. Eventually there was a twin track siding along the remainder of the quay.

Turnchapel Admiralty Wharf with a crude rail crane. August 1970. BERNARD MILLS

August 1980 with trackwork remaining.
A.R. KINGDOM

Even before the railway connection Bulteel had purchased a steam standard gauge rail crane from Priestman of Hull, their works no. A271 supplied new in 1883, a 4wVB 7 ton. Later a Thomas Smith 5 ton standard gauge 4wVB rail crane, works no. 5113 of 1896, was supplied new.

On Tuesday 7 April 1903 the Admiralty took possession of the Wharves and several acres of adjoining land for use as a coaling station for the Royal Navy. GWR papers show that 'The Admiralty have been in occupation since c1903. Permission to use sidings conveyed to them 9 January 1904'. The GWR General Manager report to the GWR Board on 29 April 1903 reported 'that wharves had been acquired by Admiralty for a coaling station'.

A seemingly unique feature of the standard gauge extension to the Wharves, was a level crossing with the narrow gauge quarry line of Sparrow, then conveying stone from the quarry to the river. An extension to the wharves in 1908 shows this note: 'This rock is being quarried by the Admiralty and removed to the coaling depot over the tramway and 'This tramway [south of the L&SWR line] is the property of Messrs Sparrow & Co. who have an uninterrupted right of way over the tramway.

Two freight services ran to the Turnchapel branch Mondays to Fridays. The morning service was to Baylys, and the afternoon went to Tunchapel Wharves.

The only passenger train to enter the site. 11 April 1959.
MAURICE DART COLLECTION

The Turnchapel branch closed to passengers on 10 September 1951 and closed to goods 20 October 1961.

One railtour visited the site on 11 April 1959 when a diesel multiple unit ran into the wharf as part of the Rail Enthusiasts Club Devon Rambler tour from Exeter St Davids.

WORKING INSTRUCTIONS SR 1934 AND BR 1960:

ADMIRALTY WHARVES

Gradient: 1 in 80 towards wharves

When a train requires to run on to the Admiralty Wharves at Turnchapel, the Porter Signalman at Turnchapel must first proceed to the wharves, obtain permission from the Admiralty authorities there for it to do so, and arrange for the gates across the single line, which are situated about 200 yards from the Turnchapel Station to be opened. He will then return to the station and accompany the train to the wharves, taking care that sufficient brake power is applied to safely control it. The load of a goods train between Plymstock and Turnchapel (Wharf) must not exceed equal to 12 loaded goods wagons and one van.

SOURCES

IRS *Rail Cranes of Devon* (draft)

Alan Lathey, D. W. Winkworth

PWDRO 2171

www.sixbellsjunction.co.uk

TNA RAIL 250/428

Royal Naval Armament Depots

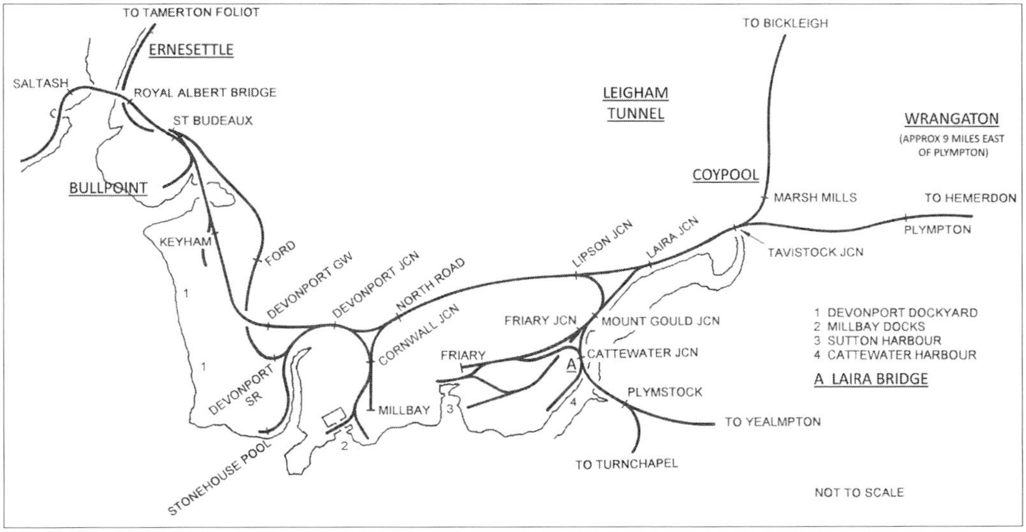

Depot locations underlined

This section includes the railways & tramways of the Royal Naval Armament Depots (RNAD) at Bullpoint and Ernesettle, and the outstations at Leigham Tunnel, Coypool and Wrangaton.

The Dockyard has always required ordnance support. The developing Royal Navy, and associated advances in weaponry through the 19th century, moved the simple (but dangerous) gunpowder and shot era into more sophisticated technology. There has always been the necessity for armament manufacture and storage adjacent to where the Fleet was stationed, hence the armament depots were established nearby. However as the Dockyard expanded over time, so early facilities had to be moved, which allowed expansion on the sites known today.

Bullpoint

The various gauges and periods in use are:
3 foot 8 inch gauge; 1853-1900
18 inch gauge; 1900-1958
Standard gauge; 1916-1985

In the mid-19th century the area of Devonport Dockyard known then as Keyham Yard (now within North Yard) was constructed, and as the Keyham Armament Magazines were too near the new Steam Factory a new location had to be

At the western end of the site. Early 20th century.
PAUL BURKHALTER COLLECTION

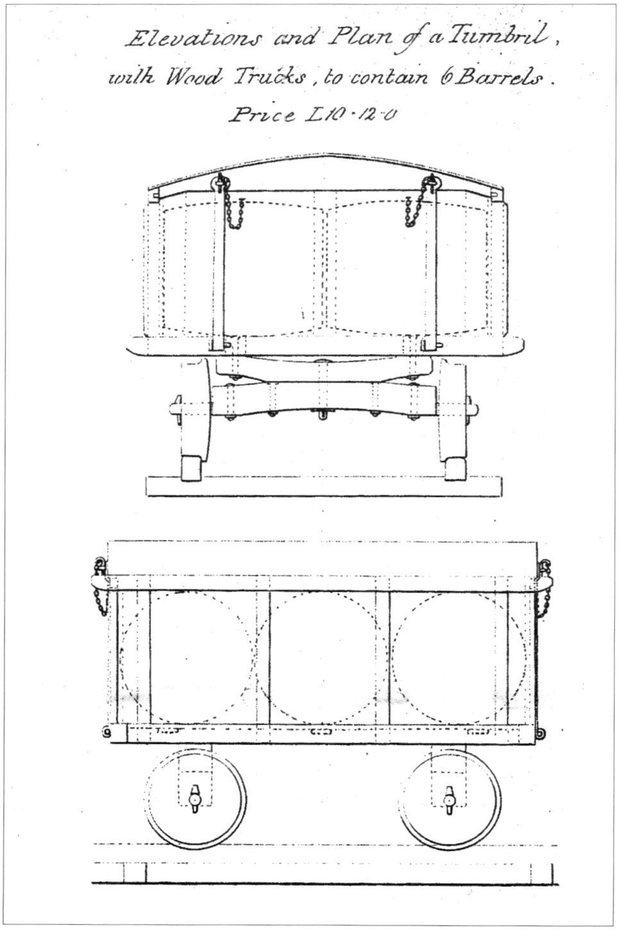

Bullpoint wagon of 3 feet 8 inches gauge.

found safely remote from the Yard. After some years of indecision new facilities were commenced in June 1850 on land purchased in 1845-6 from the Kinterbury Estate at Bullpoint, located north of Weston Mill Lake adjoining an existing powder processing site at St Budeaux with which it was to be connected by a tramway. An extensive range of buildings, many explosion protected, were erected along a very narrow stretch of shoreline, completed in the 1850s. At the outset some kind of railway was envisaged, and in 1853 a 3 foot 8 inch gauge internal tramway was laid down. It is not recorded why this unusual gauge was chosen. Hand pushed 'tumbrels' each of which could carry 6 powder barrels were built to run on the tramway. To land the materials from the water a long jetty carried two tracks of tramway which were linked with all the buildings across the site. The system of this gauge extended to 3,540 yards of track, with 29 turntables. A plan dated 15 July 1895, on a huge sheet of linen and held by PWDRO, shows the railway in great detail.

Bullpoint magazines with narrow gauge track in foreground. 1947. DEVONPORT NAVAL HERITAGE CENTRE

Bullpoint in 1947.
DEVONPORT NAVAL HERITAGE CENTRE

Bullpoint inside workshop. 1947.
DEVONPORT NAVAL HERITAGE CENTRE

GWR inspection train at the opening of main-line connection. Weston Mill Viaduct can be seen in the background. June 1916.
PAUL BURKHALTER COLLECTION

18 inch tracks in situ in 2004.
PAUL BURKHALTER

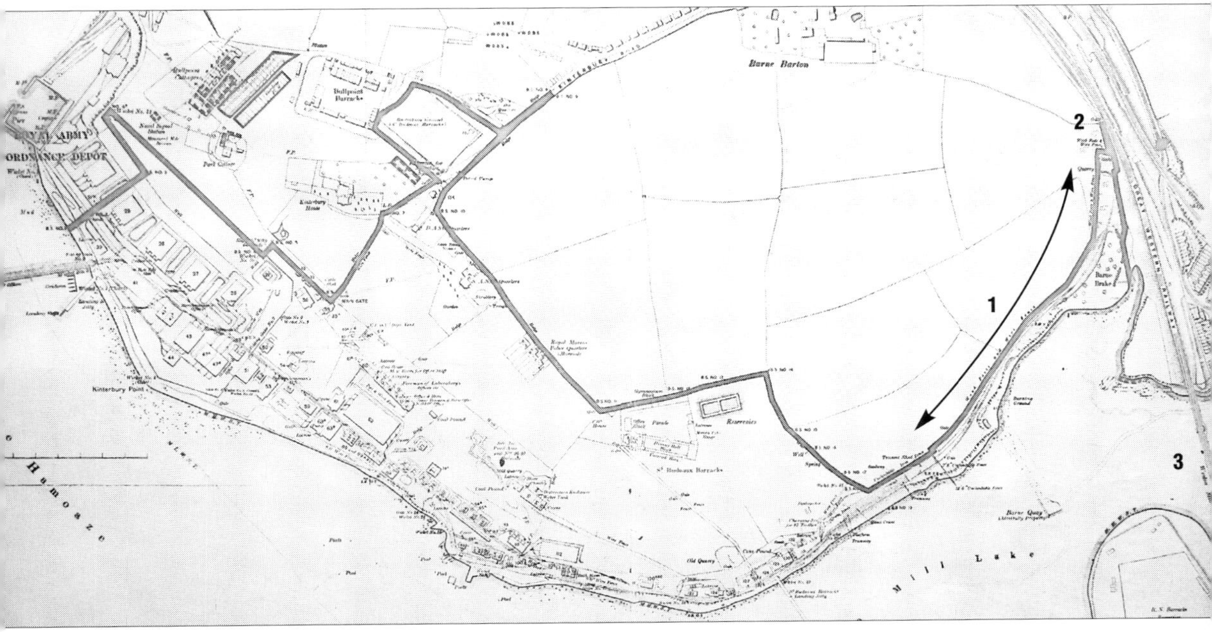

Bullpoint 1934.
1 Standard gauge branch. **2** St Budeaux Junction. **3** GWR/BR Weston Mill Viaduct.

By the mid-1870s there were concerns about the suitability of the facilities and a review in 1875 found that the tramway track was partly gunmetal, partly iron, laid on cement ways, which crumbled and was a constant dangerous source of grit (i.e. could cause sparks).

With developments in propellant new ways of operation were needed, and in 1895 a review concluded that new buildings, and the conversion of the tramway to 18 inch gauge, were necessary as the existing tramway was worn out and the 'wide gauge' made it cumbersome to operate. The 1900/01 Navy estimates included £7,100 for alterations to tramways, i.e. conversion to 18 inch gauge. A stone plaque (extant in 2014 on a wall by the four large magazines) records this: TRAMWAYS RECONSTRUCTED. GAUGE ALTERED AND LINE SOUTH OF SHELL BASE BUILT. 1900. At the same time the opportunity was taken to extend the rails to facilities previously not served. By 1934 the length of 18 inch track extended to 6,000 yards (over 3 miles), serving almost every building along the site.

5700 class 0-6-0PT 9711 at the Bullpoint Goods Shed. 2 Feb 1959. IAN D. MARKEY

For some time the matter of a main-line connection had been debated but it was the Great War that finally provided the impetus for this. A standard gauge branch from the GWR main-line at St

D7657 with a transfer goods coming off the branch at St Budeaux Jct. 28 June 1973.
© CLASSIC TRACTION

Budeaux was ready on 18 May 1916 and bought into use on 2 June. The inspection on 27 May 1916 reported that a new signal box at St Budeaux contained 13 working levers, with the branch worked 'one engine in steam' with a branch token with keys to unlock the run-round loop points. The maximum load was 20 wagons and a van, and the platform was stated to hold 12 wagons. Due to the Great War, the private siding agreement was not issued until 11 June 1924. The line descended from the main-line at 1 in 70 to a run around loop, with a transit shed and platform where the narrow gauge also had sidings. A regular freight service was timetabled, mainly an extension of the Keyham transfer goods, latterly only running as required.

The Southern and Great Western railways were adjacent at St Budeaux, directly opposite the branch junction. In the Second World War a connection between the two railways was installed to anticipate the possibility that enemy action would sever either of the lines into Plymouth. This was proven immediately it opened on 21 March 1941 as enemy action required its use for the first three days. It was also imperative to facilitate traffic from Ernesettle to the Dockyard and Bullpoint.

A site report of 1974 found: '880 yards of standard gauge branch railway maintained by the Property Services Agency, and that all but 400 feet had been recently replaced with good quality secondhand rail. One train per day enters the depot. 1,000 feet of 18 inch gauge tramway exists with one hand pushed wagon from the incinerator alongside the transit shed.'

At the closure of St Budeaux Signal Box on 2 July 1973, a new Ground Frame (Bullpoint Sidings GF) was bought into use. The bulk of the narrow gauge had fallen into disuse about 1958, and the standard gauge siding was out of use by 1985.

In 1980 two railtours ventured onto the branch, a Branch Line Society tour on 10 May, and Railway Pictorial Publications Railtours on 12 October.

RPPR Railtour from Paddington, with a DMU provided from Newton Abbot. 12 October 1980.
BERNARD MILLS

When lifted in April 1990 three-quarters of a mile of the standard gauge trackwork and four points were obtained by the Plym Valley Railway.

Bullpoint ceased to be a RNAD in the mid-1990s, and the site absorbed into Devonport Dockyard. The transit shed was demolished in March 1997.

In 1999 a review was undertaken to see if the branch was suitable for relaying to bring in construction materials for a major civil engineering project in Devonport Dockyard. In the event it proved unviable, as there were not the resources available in BR to reinstate the junction and associated signalling in the timescale required.

Locomotives

Gauge : 4ft 8½ ins

1	2	3	4	5	6	7	8	9
4	-	4w	BE	WR	-	1926	-	s/s
181	-	4w	BE	WR	-	1922	-	s/s
186	-	4w	BE	WR	-	1932	-	s/s
229	-	4w	BE	WR	-	1939	-	s/s
*	-	4w	BE	WR	737	1930	New	s/s
*	-	4w	BE	WR	1238	1938	New	(1)
*	-	4w	BE	WR	1312	1939	New	(2)
278	-	4w	DM	RH	200776	1941	(a)	s/s
279	-	4w	DM	RH	200777	1941	(a)	s/s
280	-	4w	DM	RH	200778	1941	(b)	s/s
320	-	4w	DM	RH	243397	1946	New	s/s
321	-	4w	DM	RH	243398	1946	New	s/s
322	-	4w	DM	RH	246810	1947	New	s/s

* These are presumably the same as three of the locos with running numbers 4, 181, 186 & 229.

(a) ex Colwall Tunnel Bomb Store, Herefordshire.

(b) ex Hawthorn Tunnel Bomb Store, Cinderford, Gloucestershire.

(1) to Kinnear, Moodie & Co Ltd, contrs.

(2) to Kinnear, Moodie & Co Ltd, contrs, by 11/1956.

Rolling Stock

Detailed Depot reports surviving from various years record the railway inventory. In 1904 there were 83 trucks of 18 inch gauge plus 3 hand-powered travelling cranes. In 1911 & 1913, 110 trucks and an extra crane, and in 1923 there were 162 trucks plus 3 cranes. The 1923 report makes no mention of a locomotive, though other records show 1922 for the first locomotive delivery.

Ernesettle

The various gauges and periods in use are:
2 feet 6 inches gauge: 1924-1980
Standard gauge: 1938-(extant 2017)

With further advances in naval armaments, new underground storage for depth charges was required. The topography and layout at Bullpoint was unsuitable so an outstation at Ernesettle, immediately north of the Royal Albert railway bridge, was considered suitable and lands purchased in 1921 and 1926. This comprised 100 acres of land that was reclaimed for pasture from the River Tamar in 1853 by the construction of an embankment, which was later utilised by the Plymouth Devonport & South West Junction Railway (later L&SWR) in 1887 for their new main-line to Devonport & Plymouth. The first magazines were designed in 1924 and were two pairs of tunnels into the north facing hillside at the south end of the site. Each tunnel included a 2 feet 6 inch tramway. Rails and wheels on this gauge were phosphor bronze in the magazines to prevent sparks. A short 'T' shaped jetty into the River Tamar was built for

Narrow gauge tracks to two underground magazines. 1947.
DEVONPORT NAVAL HERITAGE CENTRE

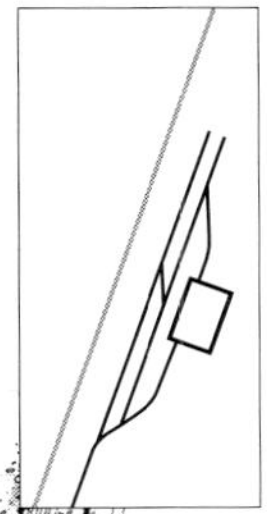

1978 transfer shed and standard gauge sidings

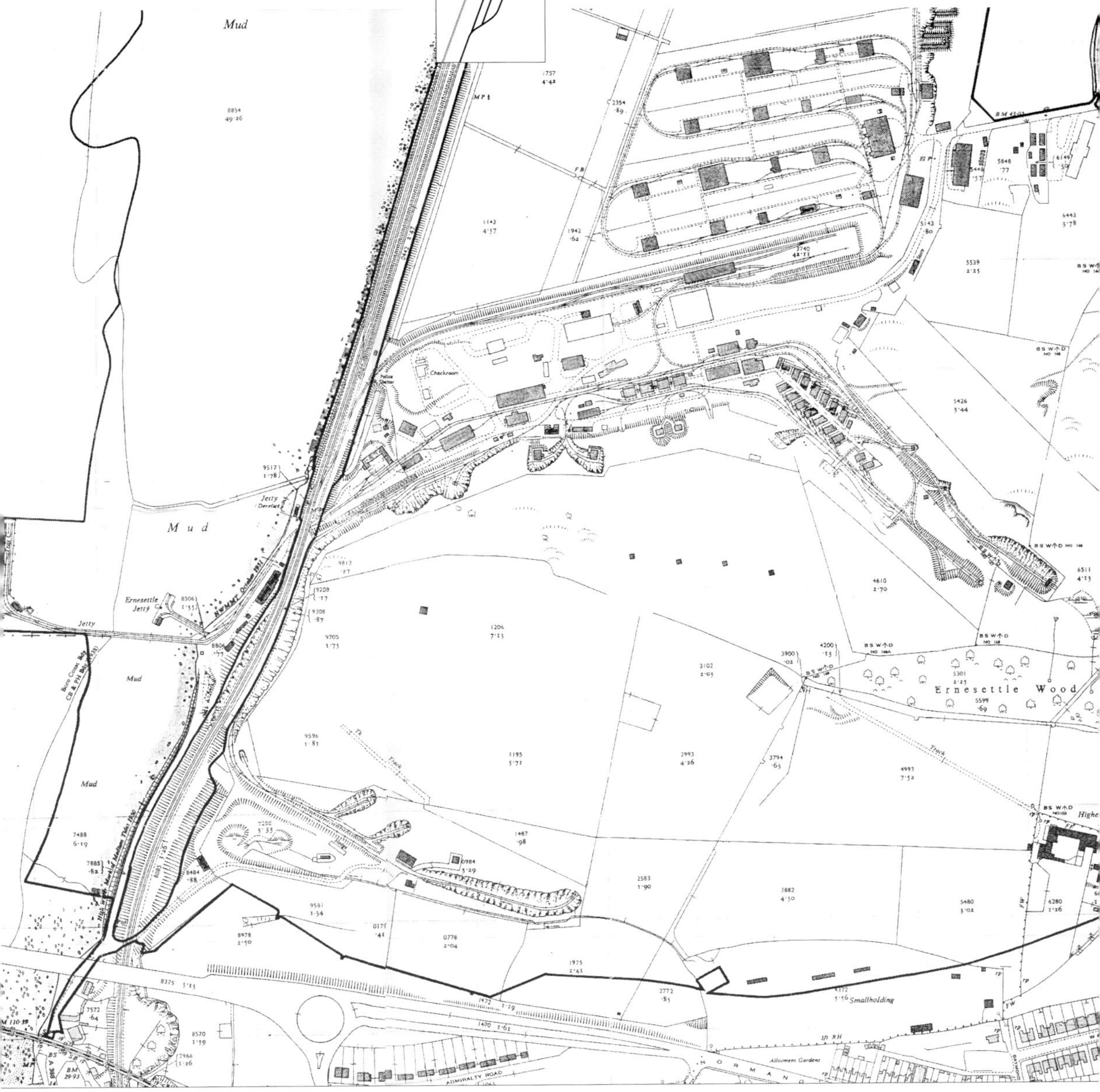

Ernesettle plan

A typical workshop building served by the narrow gauge railway. 1947.
DEVONPORT NAVAL HERITAGE CENTRE

A rail served surface magazine. 1947.
DEVONPORT NAVAL HERITAGE CENTRE

The approach to an underground magazine in 1972
DEVONPORT NAVAL HERITAGE CENTRE

water access with the tramway incorporated, and the depth charges moved by river barge between the Dockyard, Bullpoint and Ernesettle. To gain access to the jetty the SR constructed underbridge No. 705 at milepost 226. The trucks were hand-pushed until the first motive power arrived in 1938. Ernesettle was operated as an outstation of Bullpoint merely for storage until the Second World War developments expanded the facilities.

The narrow gauge line climbs the north facing hillside. October 1974.
ALAN LATHEY

The rail gate from a passing train. 9 July 2014.
NATHAN STOCKMAN

In 1938 a standard gauge connection to the SR down main-line was constructed, and bought into use on Sunday 3 July 1938. It was operated by a Ground Frame released from Bere Ferrers Signal Box. As the siding only connected to the down line, all traffic was delivered and collected by down freights. The short standard gauge branch served a Rail Transfer Shed for shipment between the two gauges and was completed in 1939/40. The transfer shed contained a central platform with standard gauge on the north side and narrow gauge on the south. Four overhead traveller cranes installed in 1941 continued in service until the 1980s. At the same time the narrow gauge system extended to serve new buildings. Demolition & Construction Ltd were the contractors for this expansion and used 2 foot gauge tramways for the construction, not without mishap as a number of accidents reported in the local newspapers show, including a labourer suffering a broken leg when 'in collision with a locomotive' in September 1938.

Bere Ferrers signal box diagram

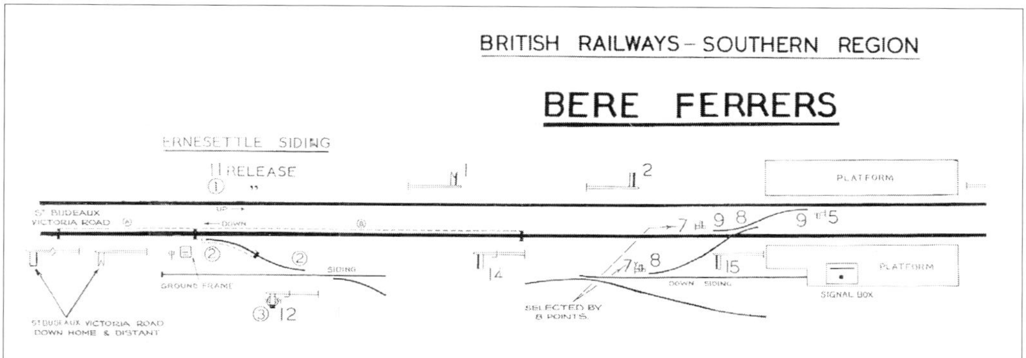

Inside the transfer shed with a standard gauge loco in the distance and narrow gauge locomotive No 4 right. 1947.
DEVONPORT NAVAL HERITAGE CENTRE

The small existing jetty was only accessible at high-tide, so by July 1941 a new 600 foot long jetty came into use designed to allow destroyers to berth. A double track extension of the narrow gauge served the new jetty head. During the war further buildings were constructed and the narrow gauge extended, usually with branches into each building. By 1945 the depot and railway was at the greatest extent, with 6 ½ miles of

Ernesettle Jetty with train, not dated.
PAUL BURKHALTER COLLECTION

A glimpse of a train on the jetty. 26 May 1956.
M. DALY, MAURICE DART COLLECTION

In the summer of 1978 a chance shot of a narrow gauge locomotive and wagon from the Tamar Bridge.
JOHN PHILLIPS

A lengthy Ernesettle transfer freight in March 1979.
BARRY JONES

narrow gauge track, and had now included the south west valley (immediately north of the present day A38), where underground magazines were constructed in 1941, together with connecting narrow gauge. Such were the differing levels leading to some higher underground magazines, a branch line had to rise up an embankment and bridges were built over the lower magazine entrances to carry the line.

A wartime proposal was to build a halt on the adjacent SR main-line, and letters were exchanged in late 1941 to explore the matter, the estimate for which was £1,500. However the Admiralty advised the SR that as most of the workforce lived in either Saltash or St Budeaux, it would not be worth installing a platform.

The Bere Ferrers Signal Box Register has survived for the 1960s, and the early part of the decade has the daily freight calling at Ernesettle between 11am and noon.

A depot report in 1974 said that all magazines had road access except Nos 7, 8, 9, & 10 which were still narrow gauge served. Two miles of narrow gauge was in daily use with 8 ton diesel locos. The standard gauge siding was 850 yards of bullhead rail with six points. There was building No. 49 for loco repair, No. 81 was the Rail Transit Shed, and No. 81A a timber loco shed. The maximum speed permitted was 5mph.

The Depot commenced supplying guided weapons in the 1960s and 1970s, which required new facilities. Increasingly roads had been built and no new narrow gauge constructed. In 1978 a new standard gauge rail served transfer shed was commenced on the west side of the depot, adjacent to the main-line, to replace the original shed, but not served by the narrow gauge. At the same time, the decision was made to cease the narrow gauge with the last use in 1980. The redundant standard gauge sidings to the original transit shed were given to the Plym Valley Railway, and most of the narrow gauge lifted in 1981.

Hunslet 6646 of 1967 was the last operational locomotive, seen here on the jetty at the end of the narrow gauge use in 1980.
PAUL BURKHALTER COLLECTION

A narrow gauge train passing under the main line. 1980.
PAUL BURKHALTER COLLECTION

Hunslet 6646 on a short train. 1980.
PAUL BURKHALTER COLLECTION

Hunslet 3133 at the Bodmin & Wenford Railway. 13 May 1990.
ROGER HATELEY, INDUSTRIAL RAILWAY SOCIETY

When the narrow gauge was removed, the Launceston Steam Railway bought a large quantity of track, pointwork, sleepers and 25 wagons. The pointwork at the east end of LSR Launceston station is from Ernesettle. Tender forms were issued for disposal of the remaining railway equipment, and a site visit in February 1981 revealed that a few hundred yards of track remained on which the stock stood. Only two locos were there: FH3831 (in full working order), and HE2245 minus engine and other parts.

Irregular main-line operations have occurred since the 1980s. On 10 April 1996 47228 delivered vans to the sidings. January 2013 four VGA/VKA vans were on site and then departed for MoD Longtown, Cumbria. The connection from the (now) Gunnislake branch has been taken into and out of use as traffic dictated, but is operational at the time of writing (2017).

Locomotives

The Railway operating instructions define these maximum loads: Hunslet locomotives Nos 1 & 2: 6 trucks loaded; Nos 3-6: 12 trucks; Ruston locomotives Nos 7 & 8: 9 trucks; Ruston locomotive No. 9: 12 trucks; Ruston No. 12: 6 trucks. On the gradients these loads were halved.

In July 1960, a shortage of standard gauge motive power led to the loan of one of the F. Hibberd Planet diesels (FH3737/1955) from Devonport Dockyard. This was moved to Ernesettle over the main-line accompanied by a BR driver, surely a unique operation. Conversely, one of the road/rail Unimogs was sent to Devonport on 23 June and 3 July 1992 for trials on train air braking. This moved by road.

A portrait of the Hunslet locomotive and crew at the end of operations. 1980.
PAUL BURKHALTER COLLECTION

Gauge : 4ft 8½ ins

1	2	3	4	5	6	7	8	9
'No.11'	(No.9)	4w	DM	RH	224349	1945	New	(2)
-	-	4w	DM	FH	3737	1955	(a)	(1)
V3	YARDNo.13	-	-	-	-	-	-	-
-	(YARD No.91)	0-4-0	DM	HE	3133	1944	(b)	(3)
52 RN 33	YARD No.90202	4w	DM Road Rail	Unimog #	-	c1978	New (c)	(4)
52 RN 35	YARD No.90202	4w	DM Road Rail	Unimog #	-	c1978	New (c)	(4)
-	MoD 253	4w	DH	TH	271V	1977	(d)	(5)
-	01 520	4w	DH	TH	322V	1987	(e)	(6)

\# Works numbers 406121 10 029450 and 406121 10 029447 respectively.

(a) ex Devonport Dockyard, c7/1960.
(b) ex RNAD, Lodge Hill, Kent, 1/1962.
(c) normally kept at Bull Point.
(d) ex MoD Ashchurch Depot, Gloucestershire, 18/3/2003
(e) ex LH Group, Barton-under-Needwood, Staffordshire, after overhaul, c10/2004; earlier MoD, Kineton, Warwickshire, MoD 274.

(1) returned to Devonport, c1960.
(2) to Royal Naval Stores Depot, Topsham, Exeter, for disposal, by 23/9/1981.
(3) to Cornwall Railway Museum, Zelah, Cornwall, 8/4/1983. Now at Bere Ferrers Station.
(4) one to Bridgwater for disposal, the other to RNAD Coulport, Strathclyde, 1996.
(5) to LH Group, Barton-under-Needwood, Staffordshire, for overhaul, c10/2004; thence to MoD
(6) to ?, by 10/2008

Gauge : 1000mm

There was no system of this gauge at this location; the locos were only stored here.

YARD No.A497	4w	DM	HE	6647	1967	(a)	(1)
YARD No.A498	4w	DM	HE	6648	1967	(a)	(2)

(a) ex Singapore Dockyard, 1971.

(1) to RNAD, Milford Haven, Dyfed, 4/1975.
(2) to RNAD, Milford Haven, Dyfed, 5/1976.

Gauge : 2ft 6ins

1	YARD No.1	0-4-0	DM	HE	2247	1940	New	(6)
2	YARD No.2	0-4-0	DM	HE	2246	1940	New	(2)
3	YARD No.3	0-4-0	DM	HE	2242	1941	New	(9)
4	YARD No.4	0-4-0	DM	HE	2243	1941	New	(9)
5	YARD No.5	0-4-0	DM	HE	2244	1941	New	(6)
6	YARD No.6	0-4-0	DM	HE	2245	1941	New	(8)
7	YARD No.52	4w	DM	RH	235737	1945	New	(10)

1	2	3	4	5	6	7	8	9
8	YARD No.53	4w	DM	RH	235736	1945	New	s/s 1972
9	YARD No.689	-	-	-	-	-	-	-
	(YARD No.45)	4w	DM	RH	268878	1952	(c)	(5)
12	-	4w	DM	RH	246794	1947	(a)	(4)
-	YARD No.85	0-6-0	DM	DC/Bg	2263	1949	(b)	(3)
-	YARD No.AD497	4w	DM	FH	3831	1958	New	(1)
-	YARD No.722	4w	DM	HE	6646	1967	New	(7)

(a) ex RNCF, Holton Heath, Dorset, c1956.
(b) ex RNAD, Lodge Hill, Kent, 10/1960.
(c) ex RNAD, Lodge Hill, Kent, 11/1960.

(1) to RNAD, Trecwn, Pembs 6/1959; returned here from RNAD Crombie, Fife, 16/12/1977; to Ffestiniog Railway Co, Portmadoc, Gwynedd, 4/1981.
(2) to Messrs Davies & Cann Ltd, Laira Bridge Road, Plymouth, for scrap, 1966.
(3) to RNAD, Broughton Moor, Cumbria, c1966.
(4) to Messrs Davies & Cann Ltd, Plymouth, 1967; scrapped 1967.
(5) to MacSalvors Ltd, Pool, Cornwall, 1/1973.
(6) to Measbury Scrap Metal Processors, Bridgwater, Somerset, c11/1975.
(7) to RNAD, Broughton Moor, Cumbria, c11/1980.
(8) to Welshpool & Llanfair Light Railway, Powys, for spares, 16/4/1981.
(9) to RNAD, Crombie, Fife, c1980.
(10) s/s after 21/6/1973.

Demolition & Construction Co Ltd
Ernesettle Contract

Work on the construction of RNAD Ernesettle for the Admiralty, 1938 - 1940.

Gauge : 2ft 0ins

1	2	3	4	5	6	7	8	9
	-	4w	DM	FH	2129	1938	New	s/s
	-	4w	DM	FH	2130	1938	New	s/s
	-	4w	DM	FH	2137	1938	(a)	s/s
	-	4w	DM	FH	2138	1938	(a)	s/s
	-	4w	DM	FH	2143	1938	New	s/s
	-	4w	DM	FH	2144	1938	New	s/s
	-	4w	DM	FH	2161	1938	New	(1)
	-	4w	DM	FH	2351	1940	New	s/s

(a) new to Demolition & Construction Co Ltd, location unrecorded – possibly to this contract, but not confirmed.

(1) later with Joseph Arnold Ltd, Leighton Buzzard, Beds, by 1958.

Rolling Stock

In 1973 an internal report stated there were 89 flat wagons, 65 box wagons, 6 brake vans and 4 miscellaneous wagons.

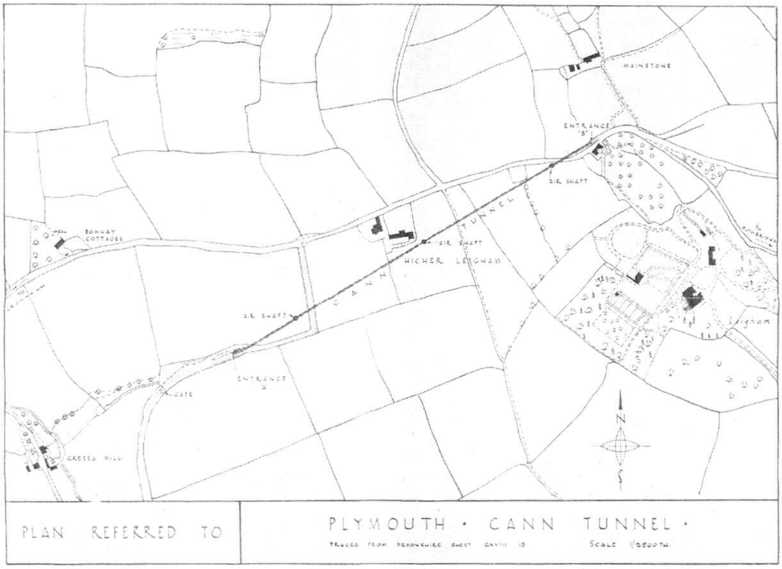

Lease for a later use of the tunnel 1953.
TNA WORK 91/302

Leigham Tunnel

(also referred to as Cann Tunnel)
Gauge (for armament use) 2 feet (?) 1944-early 1950s

The Plymouth & Dartmoor Railway was one of Britain's earliest public railways, opened on 26 September 1823. Its rare 4 feet 6 inch gauge ran from a wharf on the Plym estuary at Laira, to granite quarries 1,500 feet up on Dartmoor, near Princetown. In doing so it followed a circuitous route, with a major tunnel under a ridge close to Plymouth. Digging of

Narrow gauge tracks entering the south portal of Leigham Tunnel. 1946.
DEVONPORT NAVAL HERITAGE CENTRE

Inside the tunnel store with inset rail tracks. 1946.
DEVONPORT NAVAL HERITAGE CENTRE

the tunnel commenced in 1821. It was 620 yards long, 9 feet 6 inch high and 109 feet underground at its deepest. The P&DR fell into disuse in the 1880s. The Second World War raids on Plymouth required action to protect the population, and in 1941 Plymouth Corporation took over Cann Tunnel (their terminology) for conversion to an air-raid shelter. Tenders for this work were invited in April 1942 and nearly complete in March 1943. However by November 1944 it was considered redundant, as the threat of air-raids had passed, having seen little use. However in December 1944 the council noted that 'the Admiralty wish to use the tunnel for storage', and it was transferred over from 25 December 1944. It was used to store munitions and depth charges which commenced in October 1945. To assist the movement of such items a narrow gauge tramway was laid into the tunnel, the gauge is not confirmed but could be 2 feet ascetained from the surviving photographs. How far this line extended south of the portal is not known, however the access to the site was a lane from Plym Bridge Lane and this could have been the terminal point. When use ceased is not known, but a photograph of the portal dated 1955 shows no evidence of the rails.

Inside Leigham Tunnel about 1968.
PAUL BURKHALTER COLLECTION

The Coypool line leads off left from the Tavistock and Launceston branch. 30 Aug 1961.
R. C. RILEY

Coypool

Standard gauge: 1939-1982

The War Department purchased 30 acres at Coypool Marsh in March 1939 for the construction of an Ordnance Depot. The Army Ordnance Depot moved into Coypool in May 1941, and a sub-depot of RNAD Ernesettle opened there in March 1943. No doubt the proximity of the GWR Tavistock branch at Marsh Mills was a deciding factor for this location, and the depot was laid out to include sidings from Marsh Mills station. A letter dated 6 December 1939 gave sanction to the railway works with the GWR at an estimated cost of £8,444. The sidings & ground frame were laid in 3 November 1939, and on 12 February 1941 the ground frame was taken out of use, when operation transferred to Marsh Mills Signal Box. The private siding agreement is dated 2 January 1942. The total length of track serving the depot was ¾ mile with 7 points.

The peculiarity on the branch to the Depot was the level crossing of the 4 feet 6 inch gauge Lee Moor Tramway, which was slightly realigned

MARSH MILLS
(COYPOOL)
S. COM. O.D.

SITE:- ADJOINING NORTH END OF MARSH MILLS STATION.

ROAD APPROACH BY A. 38 AND A.37· TURNING EAST AT MAP REF. BELOW.

MAP REF. OF ENTRANCE 1" SHEET 187/520568.

REDRAWN AUGUST 1966

NOT TO SCALE

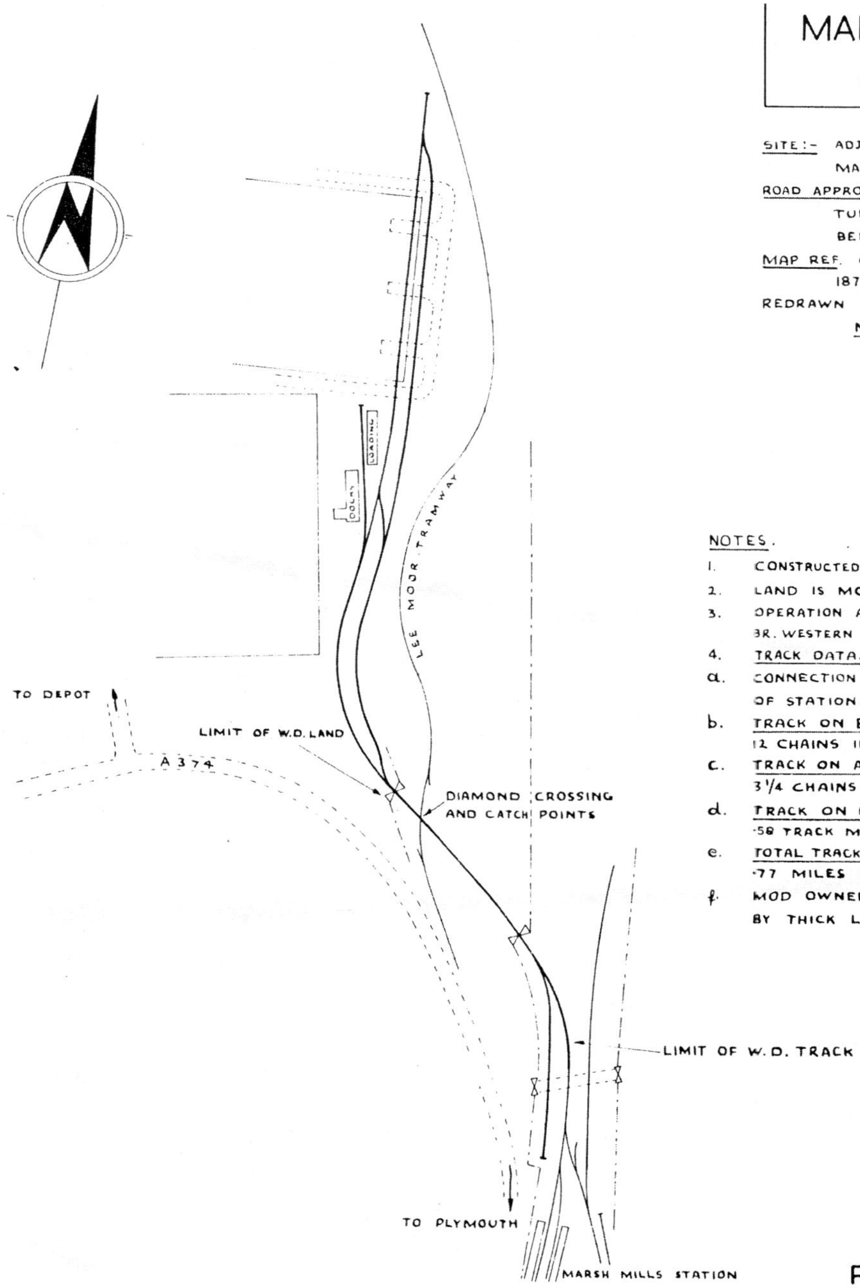

NOTES.

1. CONSTRUCTED IN 1940.
2. LAND IS MOD FREEHOLD.
3. OPERATION AND MAINTENANCE BY BR. WESTERN REGION AT MOD EXPENSE
4. TRACK DATA.

a. CONNECTION TO BR. SIDING NORTH OF STATION.

b. TRACK ON BR. LAND.
12 CHAINS INCLUDING 2 TURNOUTS.

c. TRACK ON AGENCY LAND.
3 1/4 CHAINS.

d. TRACK ON MOD LAND.
·58 TRACK MILES INCLUDING 5 TURNOU

e. TOTAL TRACK MILES SERVING DEPOT.
·77 MILES INCLUDING 7 TURNOUTS.

f. MOD OWNED TRACK SHOWN BY THICK LINE.

RLY/OP 501 MML

Former GWR 5700 class 9673 comes off the Coypool branch. 12 Dec 1950.
ALAN LATHEY

to accommodate the crossing. This was protected by catch points and signals on the LMT, controlled by a Ground Frame operated by the main-line guard or the porter from Marsh Mills. The Ground Frame and catch points were proposed to be removed in early 1959 after the cessation of use of the LMT in this location, but photographs from 1973 still shows it in situ, even though the LMT tracks had been lifted.

The Ordnance Depot closed on 15 December 1945, but the site continued as an Admiralty Stores. The branch was closed 31 March 1982, but it is thought that no traffic had passed over the line for some time before this.

Lee Moor Tramway crossing with the Coypool line. 31 March 1973.
K. JENKIN

Wrangaton aerial view 1950s.
PAUL BURKHALTER COLLECTION

Monksmoor Depot, Wrangaton
Standard gauge; 1944-1985

More storage was required as the Second World War progressed and, due to the potential high risk that was urban Plymouth, a location remote was considered necessary. A location close to the GWR main-line just west of Wrangaton Station, between Totnes and Plymouth, was selected. This sub-depot of Ernesettle was set up on 11 December 1944 after sidings were laid in 23-28 January 1944, and into use 14 March 1944. The

A freight outside the depot in 1957.
PAUL BURKHALTER COLLECTION

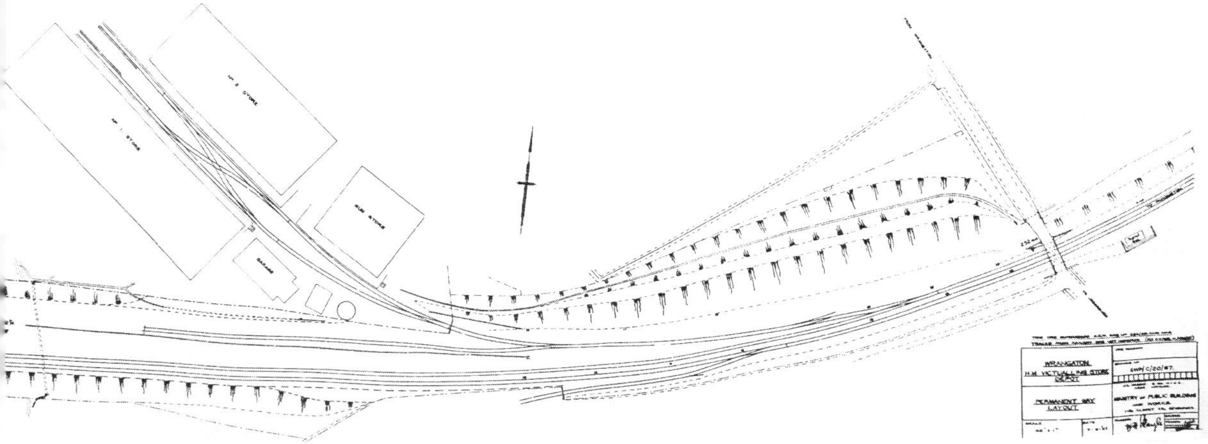

Later Wrangaton track plan in 1967.

Inspection report dated 27 August 1946 stated that the War Department required facilities to handle 40 wagons a day. The layout comprised a reception and run-round for an engine and 50 wagons and van, plus two sidings for 25 wagons each and a shunting spur for an engine and 25 wagons. The original layout of two parallel sidings was amended later when sheds were built, and the tracks laid further apart with a central crossover. The junction with the up main-line also had a facing crossover to the down, all controlled from Wrangaton Signal Box until 16 January 1966 when control for the Ground Frame went to Brent Signal Box, finally Plymouth Panel took control in December 1973. The connection was taken out of use 6 January 1985. The site closed in March 1996.

The original track layout before the buildings were constructed. 25 Oct 1945.
PAUL BURKHALTER COLLECTION

Wrangaton Depot between the store sheds. 1957.
PAUL BURKHALTER COLLECTION

Ministry of Munitions Laira Bridge (Pethicks siding)

Standard gauge used by Ministry of Munitions in the Great War.
See entry in Cattewater section.

Other locations

In passing, there are other munitions related sidings in the Plymouth area. In 1916 a siding adjacent to Lipson Junction was installed 'for munitions traffic from a nearby factory' (location not established). Also in the Second World War a siding next to Friary loco shed was laid for munitions traffic.

Sources

Devonport Naval Heritage Centre (images)

Evans, D. *Arming the Fleet* Explosion! Museum of Naval Firepower in association with English Heritage, 2006

Fergie, B. *Gunpowder to Guided Weapons* privately published by RNAD Ernesettle, 1997

Hampshire Record Office: Priddy Hard Collection

Ministry of Defence and site management records

Plym Valley Railway magazine; various issues

PWDRO: 663/47; 1023/35

TNA WO 44/307; WORK 91/302

Western Morning News; various issues

Nigel Bowman, Mike Christensen, R. A. Cooke, Larry Crosier, Bob Darvill, Stephen Dent, Chris Grove, Roger Hateley, Alan Lathey, John Lewis, John McCrickard, Bernard Mills, R. C. Riley, Superintendent Officer and Staff of RNAD Ernesettle, Don Townsley, DW Winkworth.

Construction and Contractors

Burrator Reservoir construction and enlarging (Plymouth Corporation)

The history of the water supply for Plymouth and its original satellites of Stonehouse and Devonport, collectively known as the 'Three Towns', is a fascinating one. A popular story (some say apocryphal) of the opening of Plymouth Leat by Sir Francis Drake, says he rode his horse on the bed of the leat in front of the advancing waters all the way from Dartmoor to the town. What is a fact is that the leat (a leat is an open water supply canal) was inaugurated on 24 April 1591, for a distance of 17 miles from the upper waters of the River Meavy. The site of the head weir now lies under the waters of the nineteenth century Burrator Reservoir.

In 1690 the first naval docks were constructed on the River Tamar, later to be known as Devonport. just a few miles to the west of the old town of Plymouth. As these facilities grew in size so did a new community around them, the inhabitants of which naturally turned to the neighbouring Plymouth for a supply of water from their leat. Somewhat surprisingly this was refused, and so began a long running dispute between the two authorities not resolved until Devonport had its own

Sheepstor Dam construction with rail crane.
23 March 1896.
PLYMOUTH CITY COUNCIL (ARTS & HERITAGE)

About 1894 with rail tracks on trestles serving the dam wall construction.
PWDRO 1660/2/1/2. PLYMOUTH CITY COUNCIL (ARTS & HERITAGE)

supply. Opened in 1802, Devonport Leat ran parallel to Plymouth's but obtained its water many miles further into Dartmoor. As opposed to the public ownership from the outset of Plymouth's supply the Devonport facility remained a private company until 1906. In time this open leat method was increasingly outdated, and unsafe, so Plymouth Corporation resolved to construct a new water supply scheme. A reservoir site was selected on the Meavy, with an Act obtained from Parliament in 1893, for a dam at Burrator, east of Dousland, and water carried thence by a 25 inch pipeline into town.

Work commenced on 9 August 1893 for a dam 144 feet high, and the granite obtained from a new quarry 150 yards upstream from the site (the site of which is now underwater). The reservoir site also required a second dam to close off another valley near Sheepstor, which was constructed of earth. The reservoir was officially opened in September 1898.

John Pethick was the contractor for the works, and two standard gauge steam locomotives were possibly used, no doubt to move the granite from the quarry to the dam site even though it was a short distance. They were 0-4-0ST Hunslet works number 365 of 1885, and 0-6-0ST Manning Wardle works number 818 of 1882, both of which were the type of locomotives used extensively around construction sites. However the many progress photographs do not show any locomotives although the

1923-8 enlarging. Note the stone workyard and the narrow gauge from the quarry.
PWDRO 1660/2/1/23. PLYMOUTH CITY COUNCIL (ARTS & HERITAGE)

Enlarging almost complete in 1928 showing wide gauge cranes and track across the dam and beyond.
PWDRO 1660/2/1/31. PLYMOUTH CITY COUNCIL (ARTS & HERITAGE)

cranes feature large. Also at the Sheepstor site cranes ran on rails for the length of the dam.

The three towns of Plymouth, Stonehouse and Devonport merged in 1914, and early action was taken to increase the water supply to the new larger conurbation. This was effected by enlarging the Burrator reservoir from 668 to 1,026 million gallons, by raising the water level (and hence both dam walls) by 10 feet. Work commenced late in 1923 by Corporation direct-labour and took 4½ years. This required more granite, and a quarry was opened to the south of the existing dam (still to be seen today, now a car park). From the quarry to a work area were laid 2 foot gauge tramways, with two 4-wheel Motor Rail petrol locomotives, originally built for the War Department. The works numbers were 3692 of 1924 (a rebuild of MR 1023 of 1918), and 3714 of 1925 (original loco not known). Once again cranes ran on wide gauge rail tracks, from the work area along to the dam, and across the working site. The enlarged reservoir was opened in September 1928.

PETHICK BROS LTD
MEAVY RESERVOIR CONTRACT

These locomotives are not confirmed as having been here.

Gauge : 4ft 8½ ins

1	2	3	4	5	6	7	8	9
-	-	0-4-0ST	OC	HE	365	1885	(a)	(1)
-	-	0-6-0ST	IC	MW	818	1882	(b)	(2)

(a) earlier Relf & Pethick, Lydford – Devonport (PD&SWJR) (1887-1890) contract.

(b) earlier Monk & Newell, Manchester - Wigan (LYR) (1884-1893) contract, Lancashire, and J.D. Nowell & Sons, Fairfield Junction - Chor ton Junction (MS&LR) (1889-1891) contract, Manchester.

(1) to J. Strachan, [possibly Par - St.Austell (GWR) doubling (1892-1893), Cornwall ?]; later at Stafford (LNWR) (1895-1899) contract, by 27/10/1897.

(2) possibly to Vale of Glamorgan (Barry Railway) (1895-1897) contract, South Glamorgan; later Monk & Newell, Llanishen (Cardiff Railway) (1899-1902) contract, South Glamorgan, SWANSEA.

PLYMOUTH WATER DEPARTMENT

Gauge : 2ft 0in

-	-	4w	PM	MR	3692	1924	(a)	(1)
-	-	4w	PM	MR	3714	1925	(b)	(2)

(a) ex MR, 1924; rebuild of MR 1023/1918, orig. WDLR 2744.

(b) ex MR, 3/1925; rebuild of MR ? , LOCKE No.3.

(1) to Bridgewater Bros, Ashstead, Surrey, by 11/1932.

(2) to "Contracting Plant Ltd." (?)

Cranes

In the *Western Morning News* dated 12 November 1928 is an advertisement by George Cohen (machinery dealers) for two cranes, one of which can be associated with the Burrator Contract: 'For Sale – Modern 3 ton STEAM LOCO CRANE by Smith; new 1924 25'0" jib; standard gauge. Also 8 ton ditto, by Wilson 38'0" jib. Lying at Plymouth. Cheap to avoid removal to London.'

J. PETHICK, PLYMOUTH

assumed for this contract

Gauge : 4ft 8½ ins

1	2	3	4	5	6	7	8	9
-	-	4w	VB/5t	PR	A189	1893	new	-

PLYMOUTH CORPORATION WATER WORKS

Pethick was the contractor for the 1893 construction, so why PC are shown as purchasers is not known. The 1924 cranes were for the raising of the dam height undertaken by direct-works

Gauge : 4ft 8½ ins

1	2	3	4	5	6	7	8	9
-	-	4w	VB/5t	TS	4486	1893	new	(1)
-	-	4w	VB/5t	TS	4487	1893	new	-
-	-	4w	VB/10t	TS	4489	1893	new	20ft jib
-	-	4w	VB/10t	TS	4490	1893	new	20ft jib
-	-	4w	VB/2t	TS	4995	1895	new	-
-	-	4w	VB/3t	TS	10275	1924	new	(2)
-	-	4w	VB/5t	TS	10404	1924	new	(2)

(1) to A.P.C.M.

(2) Burrator/Meavy Reservoir heightening contract

SOURCES

IRS *Rail Cranes of Devon* (draft)

PWDRO Plymouth Water Dept records 1646 and 1660

A view over the excavation for the filter bed in late 1911 or 1912.
PAUL BURKHALTER COLLECTION

Crownhill Reservoir (Devonport Corporation)

Expansion in the size of the old 'Three Towns' during the nineteenth century cumulated into the conurbation now known as the City of Plymouth. This growth resulted in storage reservoirs being built at new locations northwards along the leat supplying Devonport. In 1878 the first filter bed and reservoir was constructed on high ground at Crownhill, adjacent to one built by Plymouth two decades earlier. Further extensions were completed in 1894. Progressively, a pipeline replaced the open leat from the moor. It is worth recording that the site is still in use by South West Water today, as the principal treatment plant for Plymouth, though much of the site has been developed for other purposes.

As stated previously, the Devonport Water Company remained in private ownership, until public concern at the rates being charged resulted in the Corporation buying it in 1906 for £250,000. Almost immediately plans were made for more expansion, and the Corporation obtained an Act in 1907 for various water supply projects. Two of the proposed works were located at Crownhill for a 20,000,000 gallon storage tank and a filter bed. The estimates for these works were £39,000.

The Corporation Water Committee sanctioned the commencement of the reservoir works at their meeting on 20 July 1908, and three months later the minutes report that:

> The tender of Messrs Zadig & Co. of London for a portable railway and locomotive be accepted, as follows:
>
> 700 yards of portable railway at 4s 6d per yard; six crossings at £16 15s 0d each; 31 one yard capacity side tipper wagons at £6 10s 0d each and that the purchase of the locomotive from the above firm or Messrs Koppell [sic] be left for the Chairman or Engineer.

By 23 November 1908, Alderman E. Blackall, the Water Committee Chairman, and Mr F. W. Lillicrap, the water engineer, had visited London and called at Zadig's premises to inspect the equipment offered. Apparently the locomotive was not suitable, as the minutes record that a second-hand one was purchased from Koppel for the sum of £295.

More equipment was purchased at the beginning of 1909 when the Engineer was granted permission for the acquisition of twenty end tip

This closer view taken at the same time.
PAUL BURKHALTER COLLECTION

wagons at £8 each, and 500 yards of rails at 4s a yard. Some correspondence was exchanged with the Commanding Engineer of the neighbouring Crownhill Fort, as cuttings for the railway had been excavated into the northern glacis. He was enquiring in September 1909 as to when they were to be filled in, and was informed 'within two years'.

The excavation of the reservoir was completed on 24 October 1910, by which time a total of 143,000 cubic yards had been dug and moved. Alderman Blackall opened the reservoir on 11 October 1911. Almost immediately the filter beds work commenced, and the whole job was recorded complete at the meeting on 21 October 1912. An advertisement was then placed by the Devonport Water Engineer in the Contract Journal of 23 October 1912, offering for sale a '20hp Koppel Locomotive 2 feet gauge'. At a subsequent committee meeting held on 17 March 1913 the Engineer reported that the locomotive had been sold to Messrs J. Wardell & Co. for £160.

As to the precise identity of this locomotive all we have to show is a photograph, as the surviving Water Committee archives are silent on the matter. Unfortunately the photo is not sufficiently detailed to see the plates. However, this does allow positive identification as an Orenstein & Koppel (O&K) locomotive of 2 feet or 600mm gauge. O&K were prolific builders of such small locomotives for the construction market, so tracking down the specific engine is almost impossible. The possibility is one of a number that contractor Robert Finnegan had purchased for a Norfolk contract (works numbers 1227 (new 1903); 1229; 1272; 1273; 1343 (all new 1904)) and that could have been available in 1908 for this work. Incidentally, the high ground seen in the background are the upper slopes of the Fort, mentioned earlier, and hence locates the locomotive in the excavations for the filter bed. Therefore the photographs can be dated between the Octobers of 1911 and 1912.

Gauge : 600mm

1	2	3	4	5	6	7	8	9
-	-	0-4-0WT	OC	OK	-	-	(a)	(1)

(a) a 20hp loco, purchased second-hand, by 12/1908; origins unknown.

(1) to J. Wardell & Co, location unknown, after 23/10/1912, by 17/3/1913.

SOURCES

Harold D. Bowtell, Michael Cook, Geoff Hill, J.B. Latham, Don Steggles, Ian Thomas, Robin Weywell and Peter Witts. The minute books of the Devonport Corporation Water Committee minutes are held by the Plymouth & West Devon Record Office.

Yealm Head Water Scheme; 1928-31

In 1928 the Plympton St Mary Rural District Council obtained an Act of Parliament to empower the Council to obtain a supply of water from the River Yealm and its tributaries, to authorise the construction of works, and for other purposes. Intakes were installed in the head waters of the River Yealm on the southern slopes of Dartmoor north of Ivybridge, reservoirs and pipelines took the water down to service tanks above the villages of Brixton and Yealmpton, some seven miles away.

Lutton Reservoir. WESTERN MORNING NEWS 17 JAN 1931

Francois Cementation Co. Ltd of Doncaster were awarded the contract on 12 August 1929 for £47,724 and a new 2 feet gauge Motor Rail 4-wheel petrol loco (manufacturers No: 5047) was delivered later that year.

Certainly the construction of the reservoir near Lutton had a narrow gauge rail operation. The *Western Morning News* published a photograph on 17 January 1931 showing the construction site with narrow gauge rail tracks.

The contract was finally completed at the end of August 1931, and an advertisement in the *Western Morning News* for 6 July 1931 stated: 'For immediate disposal, 22 tons of 75lb CRANE RAILS, sundry contractors gear, &c., lying at Houndall, near Sparkwell – Apply Francois Cementation Co. Ltd.'.

Gauge : 2ft 0in

1	2	3	4	5	6	7	8	9
-	-	4w	PM	MR	5047	1929	New	(1)

(1) to Arnold Tughan & Son, builders, St.Annes-on-Sea, Lancashire, by 5/1936.

SOURCES:
PWDRO 170/69

Costain Civil Engineering Ltd, South West Water Plymouth sewer tunnel

In the early 1990s the existing sewer outfalls that discharged untreated waste into Plymouth Sound from central Plymouth were deemed unacceptable. South West Water Ltd devised a scheme to build a new treatment works at Cattedown, served by a new sewer tunnel across central Plymouth. Costain Civil Engineering Ltd were awarded the contract and commenced the 2 year work in the summer of 1996.

Shafts were sunk at Millbridge (next to Devonport High School for Boys), Millbay, Bretonside, in the former SR goods Yard at Friary (28m deep) and Cattedown. There was a spur tunnel to the Barbican. In total 4km of tunnels were driven of 2.6 and 2.74m diameter, concrete segment lined, through shillet and limestone outcrops. The tunnels were constructed in both directions from the Friary and Millbay shafts.

A 2 feet gauge railway was laid within the tunnels, and at the Friary Yard shaft was double track for about 20m either side of the shaft, then single track to the working face. Various locomotives were used over the contract period, though not all listed were on site together. The wagon fleet comprised spoil removal trucks, grout wagons and segment flats.

Gauge : 2ft 0in

1	2	3	4	5	6	7	8	9
-	263022	4w	BE	CE	5955A	1972	(a)	(1)
-	263005	4w	BE	CE	5926C	1972	(a)	(1)
-	(263023)	4w	BE	CE	B0131A	1973	(a)	(1)
-	263052	4w	BE	CE	B0142B	1973	(a)	(1)
-	263006	4w	BE	CE	B0152	1973	(a)	(1)
-	263024	4w	BE	CE	B0183A	1974	(a)	(1)
-	263025	4w	BE	CE	B0459A	1975	(a)	(1)
-	263012	4w	BE	CE	B1551C	1977	(a)	(1)
-	-	4w	BE	CE	B3686A	1990	(b)	(2)
-	-	4w	BE	CE	B3686B	1990	(b)	(2)
-	005D	4w	DH	HE	9338	1994	(c)	(3)
-	-	4w	DH	AK	47	1994	(d)	(4)

(a) earlier at Amec Civil Engineering Ltd, Swynnerton Plant Depot, Staffordshire.
(b) earlier at Thorpe Arch Plant Depot, Wetherby, North Yorkshire, 13/9/1996; originally Cairo Wastewater contract, Egypt.
(c) ex Hunslet Loco Hire, Killamarsh, Derbyshire, 28/7/1994.
(d) ex Alan Keef Ltd, Lea Line, Ross on Wye, Herefordshire, 1997.

(1) assumed returned to Amec Civil Engineering Ltd, Swynnerton Plant Depot, Staffordshire.
(2) possibly returned to Thorpe Arch Plant Depot, North Yorkshire; later to SPA Ltd, Wellingborough Plant Depot, Northamptonshire, by 21/9/1999.
(3) returned to Hunslet Loco Hire, Killamarsh, Derbyshire.
(4) returned to Alan Keef Ltd, Lea Line, Ross on Wye, Herefordshire, c24/7/1997.

Both locomotive and rail-mounted tipper at the worksite.
PAUL BURKHALTER COLLECTION

The rail-mounted tipper in action.
PAUL BURKHALTER COLLECTION

Moorcroft Quarry – Hanson/Bardon Aggregates

South Western Mining & Tunnelling Ltd were contracted to tunnel from Pit 3 to Pit 4, about 50 metres, for five water pumping mains, in 1985-6. For this work a 2 feet gauge temporary track was laid and a Ruston & Hornsby Ltd 4-wheel diesel locomotive taken to site from their plant depot near Bodmin. In 2015 this loco was extant in preservation at the Hayling Seaside Railway. In addition a rail mounted loader was used with a tipping skip.

Gauge : 2ft 0in

1	2	3	4	5	6	7	8	9
-	-	4w	DM	RH	7002/0967/5	1967	(a)	(1)

(a) ex Cottonwood Plant Depot, Nanstallon, Bodmin, Cornwall, c1985.

(1) returned to Cottonwood Plant Depot, Nanstallon, Bodmin, Cornwall, c1986.

Construction of Plymouth North-East Defences 1865-69

In the 1850s England viewed France with suspicion, and to consider this threat a Royal Commission was tasked with reviewing the defences of the United Kingdom. The 1860 report proposed, inter-alia, a line of forts to defend Plymouth and its dockyard. There were three elements to the Plymouth scheme, across the Rame Peninsula in Cornwall (later Tregantle & Scraesdon Forts), east of Plymouth Sound at Staddon Heights, and the north-eastern section between the rivers Tamar and Plym, from Ernesettle to Laira.

This latter part of the scheme comprised a line of forts on a high ridge, that gave excellent coverage over the sloping ground to the north. An Act was obtained for the purchase of, and limits of development over, a swathe of ground across the land north of Plymouth, then largely rural. The Act was accompanied by a large plan, dated August 1861, but not indicating any railway. The detailed design was by Capt Du Cane, of the Royal Engineers.

Branson & Murray, of Birmingham, were awarded the contract in 1865 – although one published account has George Baker mentioned, though this is considered to be incorrect. The spread-out nature of the work over 4½ miles of high ground, and the need to move worked stone to construct the forts and structures, led to a decision for the need of a railway. A locomotive was delivered in March 1865, and an Act (28 & 29 Vic Cap 74), dated 29 June 1865 for the 'War Dept to lay down and use a tramway or temporary railway across certain roads in the County of Devon'. It continues: 'it has been found necessary to lay down a tramway or temporary railway to connect the sites of the several Forts or Batteries, and....to use a Locomotive Engine for the drawing or propelling of trucks thereon'...'whereas the course...runs across certain Highway & Turnpike Roads in the parishes of Saint Budeaux, Tamerton Foliot, and Egg Buckland...should be sanctioned by Parliament'. Other clauses on the single page were for compensation and restoration, provision of gates and gatemen at road crossings. Disappointingly, there are no plans accompanying this Act – perhaps belying the expected temporary nature of the lines.

The locomotive that Branson & Murray purchased was from Fletcher Jennings. This builder's works book is held at the National Railway Museum, and the page for this loco tells us that it was 'begun in stock' and: 'Fletcher's Patent Mineral Tank Engine, cylinders 12in dia, stroke 20in; wheels 3ft 6in dia, four in no. coupled; wheel centres 6ft 6in' plus other technical data. It was delivered to Branson & Murray, Contractors,

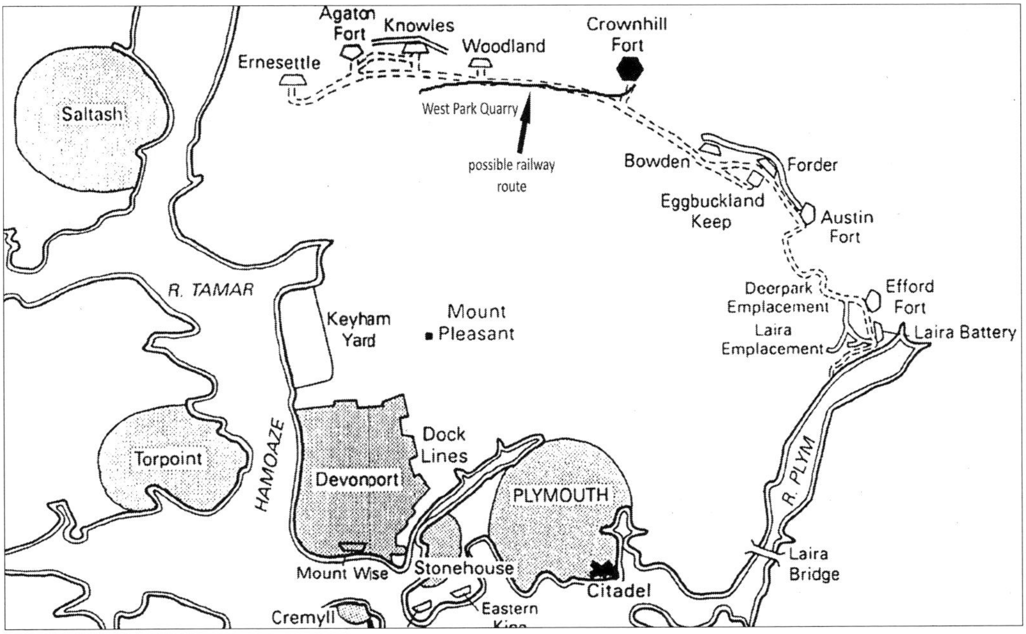

Extract from a Plan by F.W. Woodward for an Old Plymouth Society lecture 1993, with railway added.

of Birmingham, at Plymouth for new defences contract on 10 March 1865. One footnote states: 'Above was the first 12in Patent Engine'. Another footnote provides some key information: 'Capt Cox RE writes that it used to take 50 tons up 1 in 27, 300 yards long and up the Knackers Knowle Incline of 1 in 28, 450 yards – contractors wagons & temporary rails.' (Knackers Knowle is the former name for Crownhill)

Branson & Murray were bankrupt in December 1865 and the works were carried on by the Royal Engineers with direct labour.

At a meeting of the Institute of Civil Engineers 5 March 1867 'Working of Steep Gradients and Sharp Curves on Railways' was the subject. Interestingly Margary (the South Devon Railway Engineer) said he

> had received from Mr David Murray some particulars with respect to the contractors incline at the North East Defences in Plymouth. The Tank Engine used on this work was built by Messrs Fletcher and Jennings, of Whitehaven. It had four-coupled wheels 4 feet 6 inches in diameter, the cylinders were 11 inches, the tank was underneath the boiler, and the total weight of the engine was 18 tons; the gauge of the line being 4 feet 8½ inches. This engine took up the Woodlands incline of 600 yards, with a gradient of 1 in 27½, 70 tones deadweight at an average speed of 10 miles per hour; the maximum steam pressure was 110 lbs to the inch, reduced in running to 95 lbs and 90 lbs. The Knackers Knowle Bank was on a gradient of 1 in 22, for a length of 400 yards; with steam as above the engine took up 50 tons deadweight at the same average speed.

In the absence of maps showing the railway, the author has used the statements of Capt Cox and the ICE comments to plot a likely line. The incline gradients could fit with the contours along the present Crownhill Road (B3414) in the northern suburb of Plymouth, which road follows the line of the defensive earthworks between the forts. This assumption is reinforced with the boundary of the Defence Act lands including the site of a quarry at West Park.

As for the loco's subsequent life, we know only a little. The Fletcher Jennings book says: 'After Branson & Murrays failure it was taken by the Government for completion of Plymouth Defences – when those were completed in 1869 it was sold to Gadlys Iron Co., Aberdare.' Gadlys stopped making iron in 1875 and the associated Waynes Merthyr Collieries, under a succession of ownerships, had closed by February 1903.

As an aside, one other railway reference has come to light in connection with the Plymouth North-East Defences work. A local newspaper report on 3 November 1864 indicates the intention to 'construct two inclines at Laira', at the eastern end of the line of work. No doubt to hoist material from the valley floor to the site of the fort.

Gauge : 4ft 8½in

1	2	3	4	5	6	7	8	9
-	-	0-4-0T	OC	FJ	46	1865	New	-

Sources

Michael Cook

Geoff Hill

D. Moore and F.W. Woodward, Palmerston Forts Society

National Railway Museum Fletcher Jennings Loco Book

PWDRO 784/100

TNA WO 78/566

Russell Wear

Various contemporary newspapers.

John Pethick and Robert T. Relf

John Pethick was a very prominent Plymouth-born contractor and local politician (becoming Mayor of Plymouth). His company undertook many rail and civil engineering contracts between 1852 to 1914, initially locally but then further afield in the UK. Three of his railway contracts were in partnership with Robert T. Relf of Okehampton, and the histories of contractors Pethick and Relf lend themselves to be told together for a number of reasons. The most obvious is their partnership to undertake the major work of the Plymouth Devonport & South Western Junction Railway (PD&SWJR) between Lydford and Devonport, completed in 1890 after three years work. However, outside this direct connection they had similar backgrounds and upbringings, they operated over a similar period, father brought son(s) into the business, and both based themselves in Plymouth undertaking work mainly in the south-west.

Pethick made his mark on Plymouth, both politically and physically, and a number of his buildings still stand today. Relf constructed the entire L&SWR route from Sampford Courteney (east of Okehampton) through to Plymouth Friary, then upgraded most of the GWR Cornwall main-line in the eighteen years from 1894.

John Pethick was born on 19 July 1827 at Crabtree, on the Plym estuary, to the east of Plymouth. His father, Richard, was manager of the Dartmoor Granite Works (q.v.), an operation inextricably linked to the

HE365 of 1885 used on PDSWJR and possibly Burrator contracts.
FRANK JONES COLLECTION COURTESY INDUSTRIAL LOCOMOTIVE SOCIETY

Plymouth & Dartmoor Railway, which line opened just a few years before his birth and ran past the house they occupied. It is interesting that, later, John Pethick was to own the company that his father had managed and Pethick Bros still owned Swell Tor Quarry in 1910.

He left school at 12, and the following year went into employment as a trainee carpenter in Mr Pope's shipbuilding yard at Turnchapel, on the other side of the Plym. At the early age of 19 he married Maria Oram at Stoke Damerel Church, Plymouth, on the 27 December 1846. They went onto have 9 children, one of whom (their first) died in infancy.

By the age of 21 he was working on building the Esplanade, a splendid row of houses along the crest of Plymouth's Hoe, for a Mr Phillips. In 1852, at 25, he went into partnership with Benjamin Call, as builders and contractors, which arrangement lasted until 1871.

After Call and Pethick dissolved the partnership in about 1871 (though some works are recorded in joint names until the end of 1872, no doubt finishing off work already in progress) Pethick's career blossomed. The works he engaged in were many and diverse. Notable projects include the Vale of Rheidol Railway from Aberystwyth, foundations and piers for London's Vauxhall Bridge, the widening of London Bridge, and the grandiose Plymouth Art Gallery & Museum. Many of his Plymouth works survive today. In 1876 Pethick's address was Norley Buildings, Plymouth and for many years his depot was at Laira Bridge, on the same site as the granite works that his father managed. The depot was rail connected to the L&SWR Cattewater branch The 1881 census records him as employing 576 men.

John Pethick was a director of Plymouth Tramways Co., formed in 1889 to take over the ailing services on the recently opened Millbay to Mutley Plain line provided by steam trams. His company stopped the unpopular steam service and substituted horse drawn trams before selling out to the Corporation in 1892 for £12,500.

In August 1886 he and Robert Relf jointly won the PD&SWJR Lydford to Devonport job. The reasons for them coming together are not known, no doubt they came to know each other by working in the same area, even possibly bidding against each other. John Pethick Jnr attended the ceremony for the cutting of the first sod of the PD&SWJR on 29 March 1887 at the site of Shillamill Tunnel near Tavistock. The joint working arrangement between Relf and Pethick also existed for the Plymstock and the Turnchapel lines, and was only for these three specific contracts. They both undertook contracts separately under their own names through this period.

Outside his construction activities, Pethick was representing the Conservatives on Plymouth council by 1874. He served as Mayor

between 1898 and 1900, as well as being appointed a Justice of the Peace. Alderman Pethick was often referred to as 'Honest John', though it was said sometimes his 'honesty' landed him in trouble for its forthrightness.

Early work on Burrator Reservoir in 1893
PWDRO 1660/2/1/2. PLYMOUTH CITY COUNCIL (ARTS & HERITAGE)

Four of his sons followed him into the business in partnership, the firm becoming known as Pethick Bros from sometime in the late 1880s. They were: John Richard, Arthur Henry, Benjamin Herbert ARIBA and Nicholas Frank, whilst Ernest George also served the family firm. Two other sons became, respectively, a doctor (Charles Stuart) and a veterinary surgeon (Sydney Robert), and his one surviving daughter, Edith, married Clarence Spooner, whose family were owners of one of Plymouth's largest shops. Arthur is recorded as being the superintendent of much work in Devonport Dockyard, including the laying of the railway through the tunnel that connects North and South Yards. Arthur's son, Harold W., left for South Africa between 1901 and 1907, where he carried on as a railway contractor until sometime in the 1920s.

John Pethick died aged 76, after an accident on 29 March 1904 when his horse drawn carriage ran out of control with him at the reins in Lockyer Street, in central Plymouth. The sons continued as Pethick Bros, until the last recorded contract in 1910. In June 1914 an auction sale was advertised, on the instructions of the Receiver, for all the contractors' plant, machinery, etc, at the company's works at Laira Bridge. This included three 4 wheel coupled locos, without identifying the makers.

Robert Thomas Relf was born in Southampton on 24 May 1833, the son of a millwright, and of a large and very old Cranbrook (Kent) family stretching back to the 1600s.

After running away from school at the age of 12 he worked for Betts & Son on the construction of the Chester & Holyhead Railway (1845-1848), the GNR Peterborough to Boston and Lincoln line and the 'Doncaster loop line'; then on to Peto, Brassey & Betts' London, Tilbury & Southend Railway contract as assistant to the agent, Thomas White. From 1858 to 1868 he worked with the well-known contractors Smith & Knight on various railways, in Lincolnshire, on the Paignton branch (his first connection with Devon), the Metropolitan Railway and the Mid Kent and Addiscombe lines.

His first job as a contractor in his own right, in 1868, was the maintenance of the Doncaster to Gainsborough line, on which he had worked for Sir John Fowler during its construction. During this period he visited Sardinia to report on the cost of completing the Royal Sardinian Railway. In 1871 he contracted with the Devon & Cornwall Railway Co. to build a line the short distance from Okehampton Road (later Sampford Courtenay) to Okehampton. At the opening banquet, in responding to the toast 'the Contractor', he said, 'Gentlemen, I cannot make you a speech, but if you find me the money, I will build you another railway.' This obviously worked, for shortly after he continued the line westward to Lydford, including the Meldon Viaduct. A plethora of Devon jobs followed: the Holsworthy branch, Sidmouth Railway, Plymouth North Road to Devonport (L&SWR), works at Stonehouse Pool, and Laira to Friary for the L&SWR. To facilitate these works he became resident in Okehampton from 1870 to 1880, before going to London for 7 years (offices at 26 Parliament Street, Westminster, and a residence at Meldon House, Ravensbourne Park – note the Devon connection).

However, the winning of the very large PD&SWJR contract between Lydford and Devonport in 1886 caused him to move to Plymouth, where he remained for the rest of his life. It was for this job that he and John Pethick came together.

In about 1895 Relf took his eldest son, George Robert Relf, into business with him and proceeded as R. T. Relf & Son. They undertook the GWR Saltash to St Germans deviation (a plaque on St Germans viaduct records Relf & Son as contractor), replaced a number of Brunel's Cornwall Railway timber viaducts with stone structures, and carried out many other works in the counties of Devon and Cornwall. Further afield they built the Meon Valley Railway between Fareham and Alton, and two slipways at Pembroke Dock for the Admiralty.

He died, aged 83, on 12 December 1915 at 17 Portland Villas, Plymouth. In May 1916 'after decease of R. T. Relf' two 6 coupled and three 4 coupled locomotives were offered for sale at Wearde, near Saltash. This appears to have been a depot, no doubt a facility remaining upon completion of the adjacent GWR main-line deviation. It is conjectured that there may have been an opportunity for further work, as the GWR were proposing a branch to Callington at the time, which would have left the main-line at Wearde. In the event the powers lapsed and nothing was done.

His son George would appear to have carried on the business until about 1925 and he died at Mannamead, Plymouth on 21 August 1930, aged 71.

Other contracts would have used locomotives but these have not been recorded.

SOURCES & ACKNOWLEDGEMENTS

Binding, J. *Brunel's Cornish Viaducts* Pendragon Books 1993

Andre Evans FICE (access to the ICE Archives).

Fryer, S. *Building of the PD&SWJR* author 1997

Roger Hateley

Gary Hicks (Plymouth shipping history)

Geoff Hill

John Lewis (research at TNA)

Plymouth University Library.

Chris Relf of the Relf Society;

Russell Wear

Peter Witts

The Frank Smith Collection at the Institution of Civil Engineers.

The Industrial Locomotive No 108, Industrial Locomotive Society 2003

J. Pethick Plymouth area railway contract locomotives:

1	2	3	4	5	6	7	8	9
PHYLLIS	-	0-4-0ST	OC10x15	HE 365/1885	-	-	-	(1) (2)
BEATRICE	-	0-4-0ST	OC10x15	HE 366/1886	-	-	-	(1)
OXTED	-	0-6-0ST	IC12x17	MW 597/1877	-	-	-	(1)
-		0-6-0ST	IC12x17	MW 818/1882	-	-	-	(2)

R.T. Relf Plymouth area railway contract locomotives:

BEE	-	0-4-0ST	OC11x	HH				(1)
LIVELY	-	0-6-0ST	IC13x18	MW 291/1870	-	-	-	(1)
CROYDON		0-6-0ST	IC12x17	MW 527/1874	-	-	-	(1)

(1) PD&SWJR Lydford-Devonport, 4/1887-6/1890

(2) Burrator Reservoir, 1893-4 (possible –see text)

PETHICK and RELF (P&SWJR construction)
Gauge : 4ft 8½in

1	2	3	4	5	6	7	8	9
-	LIVELY	0-6-0ST	IC	MW	291	1871	(a)	(1)
-	OXTED	0-6-0ST	IC	MW	597	1877	(b)	(2)
-	CROYDON	0-6-0ST	IC	MW	527	1874	(b)	(3)
	-	0-4-0ST	OC	HE	365	1885	(c)	(4)
-	ALICIE	0-4-0ST	OC	HE	366	1886	(c)	(5)
-	BEE	[0-4-0ST	OC?]	HH	-	-	(d)	(6)
-	JUBILEE	0-4-0ST	OC	MW	990	1887	(e)	(7)

(a) ex Falkiner & Tancred, Didcot, Newbury & Southampton Railway (1879-1884) contract, Berkshire.

(b) ex J.T. Firbank, East Croydon – East Grinstead (SER & LBSCR) (1880-1884) contract, Surrey.

(c) ex Holme & King, Shenfield - Wickford (GER) (1883-1888) contract, Essex.

(d) ex George Young, Engineer for Ryde & Newport Railway, Isle of Wight, (to R.T. Relf, Okehampton, 6/1888 – use on this contract assumed).

(e) originally Wm Mousley & Co, Skipton-Ilkley (Midland Railway) (1885-1888) contract, North Yorkshire; (owned by Relf in the 1888-1893 period – use on this contract assumed).

(1) to J.T. Firbank, Knights Hill Coal Wharf (LNWR) (1889) contract, Dulwich, London; later J.T. Firbank West Hampstead - Marylebone (GCR) (1894-1899) contract, London.

(2) to Pethick Bros, Devonport; later to Crawshay Bros (Cyfartha) Ltd, Merthyr Tydfil, Mid Glamorgan.

(3) to R.T. Relf & Son, contractors.

(4) later John Strachan, Rotherham Main Colliery branch (GCR) (1898-1899) contract, Yorkshire (WR).

(5) later Pethick Bros, Blagdon Reservoir (Bristol Corporation) (1897) contract, Somerset; later to Victoria Wharves Ltd, Plymouth, by 11/1917.

(6) "Railway & Shipping Contractor", 23/4/1891 gives "Ward & Chowen to auction, on 27/4/1891, at yard, Devonport, re Relf & Pethick, P.D.& S W.J.R, plant including three locos: 11in four-wheel loco by HH, 13in, six-wheel loco LIVELY by MW and 12in six-wheel loco OXTED by MW." This suggests that the HH loco known to have been owned by Relf was used on this job. Disposal of this loco not known.

(7) later Henry Lovatt, Ampthill (Midland Railway) (1893) contract, Beds.

Contractors associated with main-line railway work

Lucas & Aird

Plymstock to Yealmpton railway for the GWR. Work started on 30 December 1895, and the line opened on 15 January 1898. At least one locomotive was used, seemingly named Lady Morley for the opening day ceremonies.

S. Pearson & Son Ltd

Doubling the GWR main-line between South Brent and Ivybridge 1890-1893. 7 feet 0¼ inch gauge: two GWR loco's were purchased and resold after the works back to GWR.

Gauge : 7ft 0¼in

1	2	3	4	5	6	7	8	9
2172	OWL	0-4-0WT	IC	AE	900	1873	(a)	(1)
2174	GOAT	0-4-0WT	IC	AE	901	1873	(a)	(1)

(a) ex GWR, 11/1890.

(1) resold to GWR, 6/1893 and later rebuilt to 4ft 8½in gauge.

Pittrail Ltd

Lifting of the Marsh Mills to Tavistock branch in 1964

Gauge : 4ft 8½in

1	2	3	4	5	6	7	8	9
-	-	4w	DM	RH	198324	1940	(a)	(1)

(a) prev. F. Watkins Ltd, Coleford, Gloucestershire; orig. Air Ministry.

(1) to Aldridge Plant Depot, Staffordshire, by 1/1965; later scrapped there.

Townsend, Watson & Gates

Construction of the GWR Mount Gould to Cattewater Junction spur
The locomotive listed below is known to have been owned by TW&G and so may well have been the 11inch one advertised for sale on this job.

Gauge : 4ft 8½in

1	2	3	4	5	6	7	8	9
	BARROW DOCKS No.4	0-6-0ST	IC	MW	174	1865	(a)	(1)

(a) earlier Furness Railway, Barrow Docks (1872-1879) construction, Barrow in Furness.

(1) 11in loco for sale by auction on 16/7/1897; MW 174 to R.T. Relf & Son, Westleigh Quarry (1898) contract; later with Pauling & Co Ltd, High Wycombe (GWR/GCR Joint) (1901-1905) contract, Buckinghamshire.

Clay train at Laira, on the old Plymouth & Dartmoor Railway section of the Lee Moor Tramway. ALAN KITTRIDGE

Other

Plymouth & Dartmoor Railway and The Lee Moor Tramway

The full stories of these two lines in Plymouth has been well told elsewhere, and what follows is a summary of the history of these railways. Both were built to the unusual gauge of 4 feet 6 inch.

Sir Thomas Tyrwhitt had been developing the waste of Dartmoor, for twenty years including building Prince's Town, named after the Prince of Wales, later King George IV, and the prison there in 1809. The buildings lay deserted after the end of the war with France (which prisoners it housed) in 1815. To further progress his aims, he planned to reclaim the land, and to this end proposed a railway from Plymouth to Princetown in November 1818. Imports would be materials for the farming activities and exports of granite from the quarries and peat.

On 2 July 1819 Royal Assent was given for the Plymouth and Dartmoor Railway Act, authorising the construction of a line from Crabtree, in the parish of Eggbuckland, to Princetown. In 1818 it was surveyed by William Shillibeer of Walkhampton and an estimate of £27,788 was put forward for the railway. William Stuart, who was superintendent of the Breakwater Works, was chosen as the engineer, whilst Hugh Mackintosh of London, the contractor. The iron rails were supplied by Messrs Bailey & Company, also of London. The second Act, on 8 July 1820, gave authority for an extension to Sutton Pool, along with a short branch to Martin's Wharf on the Cattewater, just below Laira Bridge. The original survey by Stuart for the line between Crabtree and Jump (now known as Roborough) proved unworkable, so a third Act, dated 2 July 1821, allowed the line to deviate, following contours, with a 620 yard tunnel on that section. A new engineer, Roger Hopkins, was brought in to progress the deviation. The work was estimated to cost £12,200. However the final cost was said to be £66,000, far in excess of the original estimates, which was to trouble the railway for all its life.

The Plymouth & Dartmoor Railway was opened on 26 September 1823. The gauge was 4 feet 6 inches, which henceforth became known locally as the 'Dartmoor' gauge. The line was 25 miles, 2 quarters and 6 chains long, of single track throughout with passing sidings. It ran from King Tor, just short of Princetown, to Sutton Pool, Plymouth. It was horse worked for all its working life. King Tor Quarries were worked by two brothers, John and William Johnson. The Plymouth and Dartmoor Railway company had now run out of money, and the Johnson brothers helped financially with the completion of the line into Princetown. In return they took out a mortgage on the line but as the Company could not pay the interest on it, they allowed the Johnsons to transport their granite free of charge. There was no other traffic on the line to pay the running costs, so it became virtually a private railway for the Johnsons. A branch of the Plymouth & Dartmoor Railway was opened from Crabtree to the Cann Quarry Canal basin at Marsh Mills on 20 November 1829 (or 20 January 1830 – reports vary), then extended to the quarry along the towpath in 1833 and worked until about 1855. Another branch opened in 1833 to Plympton that was bought by the South Devon Railway in 1847 and closed for the construction of their new line from Totnes to Plymouth. This main-line also resulted in the P&DR (later the LMT) Dartmoor gauge crossing the broad and standard gauge on the level at Laira

By an Act of Parliament, dated 19 June 1865, the surviving Johnson brother, William, was given £75,000 worth of 5% preference shares in exchange for the mortgage. This brought matters back into the control of the Company and within a few years the revenue from transporting the granite enabled them to relay much of the line in 1873 and 1874. Meanwhile the SDR had bought the line to Sutton Pool and converted it to mixed broad and Dartmoor gauge in 1853, which lasted until 1869. In 1883 much of the top section of the railway, above Yelverton, was used by the Princetown railway as the trackbed of the standard gauge line to Princetown. This left the remainder with very little traffic and the line ceased to be used. Hence the P&DR ceased to be a working railway above the junction with the Lee Moor Tramway (q.v.).

At the end of the 19th century the P&DR company became a vehicle for the L&SWR to promote branches to the east of Plymouth, which story is beyond the scope of this book.

In 1916 all the Plymouth & Dartmoor railway track was removed, except that between the Rising Sun Inn at Crabtree and Sutton Harbour, which remained as part of the Lee Moor Tramway.

Lee Moor Tramway

The P&DR branch to Plympton was used to transport the clay bought down from Lee Moor, and when it was closed for the South Devon Railway, an alternative was required. Lord Morley had an agreement with the broad gauge South Devon & Tavistock Railway for a Dartmoor gauge branch to be built to Lee Moor, however in the event the SD&TR 'gifted' the line to Morley in June 1856 to rid themselves of the obligation. Work had been previously started, but the contractor employed did such a bad

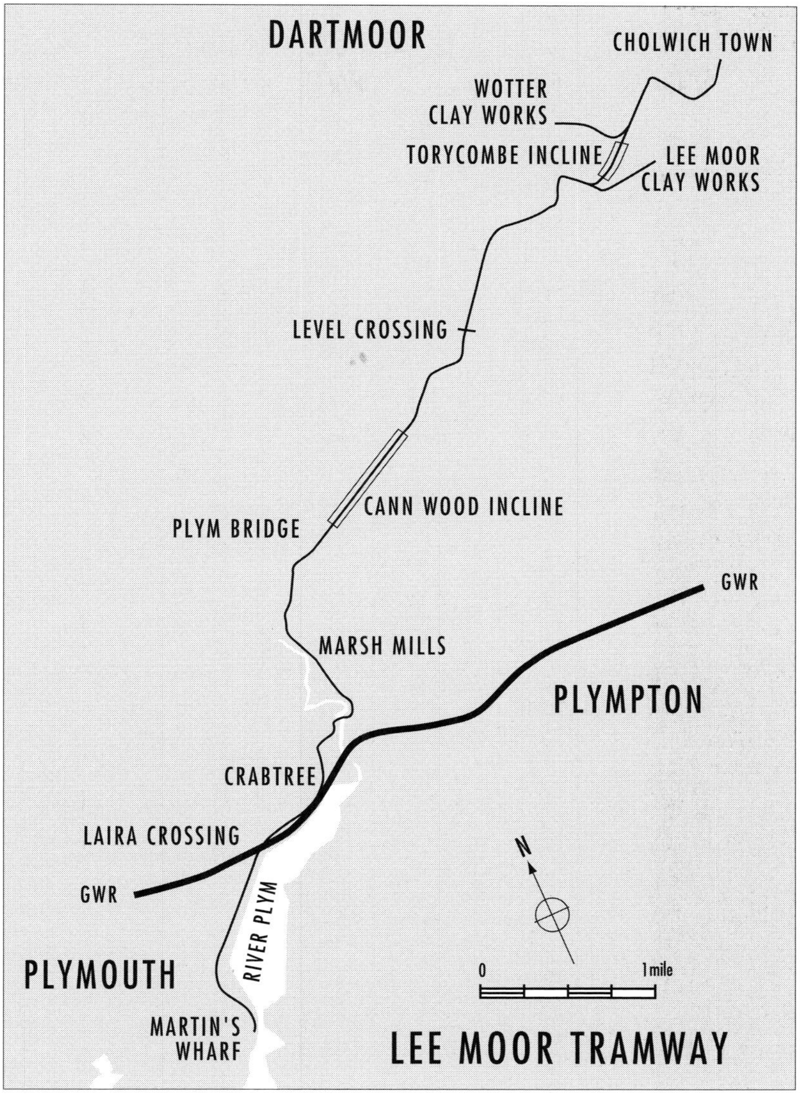

job that it was unsafe to operate. After the South Devon & Tavistock Railway handover to Lord Morley, a new contractor was used and the line finally opened 24 September 1858. Firstly horse worked, the section from the top of Cann incline to Torycombe was relaid with heavier rail, and locomotive haulage introduced from 1899. From 1919 English China Clay took over the workings at Lee Moor and operated the railway. This continued up until the Second World War, but the construction of a pipeline to convey clay slurry to the Marsh Mills clay works, and reduced clay mining, led to decreasing use of the Tramway. It is likely that the last use of the line at Lee Moor was 31 December 1945.

To retain the right of way, especially over the main-line at Laira, a

Roy Taylor stands beside restored *Lee Moor No2* in 1968.
MICHAEL MESSENGER

short horse drawn train was occasionally run between Weighbridge Cottage at Marsh Mills, and Maddocks Concrete Works on the Embankment, but this ceased with the final working of a single wagon on 26 August 1960.

Locomotives

Two engines were obtained from Peckett & Sons in Bristol in 1899. Works numbers 783 and 784, they were named *Lee Moor No. 1* and *Lee Moor No.2* respectively, being delivered on 24 March and 6 April 1899. They were 0-4-0ST weighing 13 tons 15 cwt and were built from standard designs to 4 feet 6 inch gauge.

After cessation of the use of steam locomotives in 1945, the two engines were locked in the shed at Torycombe where they remained until members of the Plymouth Railway Circle formed the Lee Moor Tramway Preservation Society in 1964. Both locomotives were preserved, and in 2016 *Lee Moor No.1* is at the Wheal Martyn Clay Museum near St Austell, and *Lee Moor No.2* in a purpose built store at Buckfastleigh Station.

SOURCES AND FURTHER READING:

Shepherd, E.R. *The Plymouth & Dartmoor Railway and The Lee Moor Tramway,* ARK Publications 1997

Taylor, R.E. *The Lee Moor Tramway – A pictorial record,* Twelveheads Press 1999

Gauge : 4ft 6in

1	2	3	4	5	6	7	8	9
LEE MOOR No.1		0-4-0ST	OC	P	783	1899	New	(1)
LEE MOOR No.2		0-4-0ST	OC	P	784	1899	New	(1)

(1) withdrawn 11/1945; to Lee Moor Tramway Preservation Group, at this site, 1964.

Minor locations

Phoenix Marble Works & Sawmills, Millbay

A notice advertising an auction of plant on 6 March 1909 in connection with the dismantling of the Phoenix Marble Works and Sawmills at Millbay, Plymouth, included a standard gauge four wheel locomotive. The location, whilst nearby to Millbay Station of the GWR, was never rail connected, nor are rail tracks showing on the Ordnance Survey. There are two possible explanations: either the auctioneers included the item for convenience but it was actually elsewhere, or the works had an old locomotive on site in use as a stationary boiler.

Baggage tramway on Millbay Pier, pictured in 1988.
ALAN KITTRIDGE

Millbay Pier baggage tramway

Arguably a self-contained outpost of the GWR, a 2 feet 6 inch (estimated) tramway was laid out in around 1900 to serve the ocean liner terminal's baggage and mailbag handling on Millbay Pier in the GWR's Millbay Docks. Loaded trucks were hand pushed from a loop line on the pier around to East Quay and into Baggage Inspection Rooms Nos 1 and 2, where they looped around the inspection tables and rejoined the 'mainline' outside. After the Second World War the tramway was superseded by electric-tractor hauled trolleys that clattered noisily across the old rails and cobble stones. Remains of the tramway were in evidence until the area was re-developed in the 1990s.

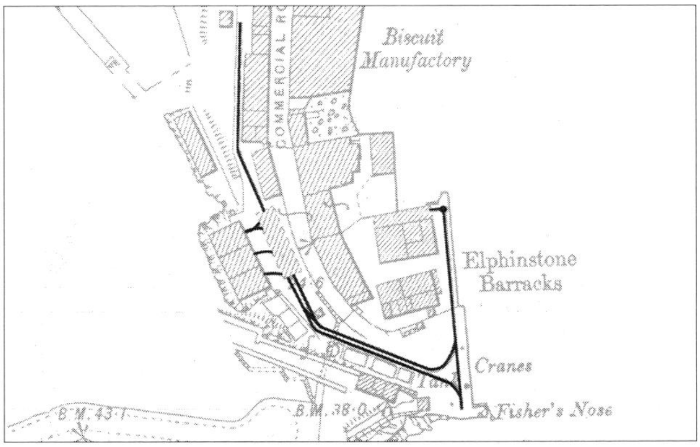

Elphinstone 1895

Elphinstone Emigration Depot

In the mid-19th century emigration to the colonies was a burgeoning activity. In 1847 some old warehouses at Elphinstone Wharf, below the Citadel at the entrance to Sutton Harbour were made into a Government Emigration Depot. By 1897 the depot had closed and became a Royal Engineers Torpedo

Depot. The 1895 and 1914 OS show two layouts of narrow gauge tramways. It is hypothesised that the emigration depot period was to move passengers luggage to the quay, and the torpedo depot for the weapons.

Drakes Island Jetty

A 2 feet or 2 feet 6 inch track was laid along the jetty sometime before 1963 and was extant in 1979. At the time the island was in use as a youth training centre. Presumably a hand-pushed wagon was utilised to move stores landed from vessels.

Drakes Island Jetty tramway.
PAUL BURKHALTER COLLECTION

Building contractors temporary tramways

- Maurice Dart recalls that in 1939 he observed 2 feet gauge temporary tracks laid in Normandy Way in connection with the construction of police accommodation.
- Kier Ltd utilised a narrow gauge hand worked tramway in a construction project in a very restricted location within Devonport Dockyard in the early 2000s.

Mines

Dartmoor is rich in minerals, which have been exploited since time immemorial. Mines in the area covered by this book occasional used very short tramways to move the ores between facilities.

Examples are:

- Wheal Sydney in Fernhill Wood in the Tory Brook valley north of Newnham Park, Plympton, where the dressing floor was connected to the shaft by a tramway in the period of operation 1850-80.
- Wheal Mary Hutchins Mine near Hemerdon, an arsenic and tin mine from 1880, obtained a licence from the landowner (the Strodes of Newnham Park) for a burning house and tramway. This became part of the British Arsenic Mines in 1896.

Private Sidings

Private sidings were laid off the main-lines to serve lineside warehouses, factories, etc.

- At Crabtree a development adjacent to the main road between Plympton and Plymouth was built in the early 1960s. It was also adjacent to the main-line just to the west of Tavistock Junction, and a

Crabtree with D2140 passing. Crabtree siding is on the left. 1968.
BERNARD MILLS

single siding was installed 500 feet long with a 300 feet trailing dead-end. The trailing junction with the up line was bought into use on 24 November 1964. Sometime in 1967, two additional sidings parallel with the first were installed. The adjacent warehouse was operated by Drake Carriers Ltd. In later years some preserved rolling stock was stored here. The 1993 BR rule book contains specific instructions about operating this siding, the maximum speed being 15mph, and that no locomotive or vehicle shall be placed on the connecting line between the main-line and the sidings. The sidings were out of use by the early 1980s, and the junction with the main-line removed.

- M.Thomas Distribution – Friary. A single siding installed August 1966 on the Friary Locomotive Shed site accessed from the Plympton branch adjacent to Lucas Terrace Halt. It was still in use in 1990.
- Plymouth & Stonehouse Gas Light & Coke Co. Ltd – Located on the Sutton Harbour branch, adjacent to North Quay Branch Junction. There had been a gas works here since 1853, but it was not until 1922 that a purpose built siding was installed. The private siding agreement was dated 16 July 1919, and the double ended siding bought into use 14 December 1922. The works were closed on 31 July 1968. The branch and associated sidings were closed 3 December 1973. On the loading bank was an electric standard gauge rail crane manufactured by Thomas Smith, Rodley of 5 tons works number 9923 and delivered new in 1922. There is no sign of the crane in a photograph dated 1962.
- H. Ede & Sons – Cement Works siding adjacent to Sutton Harbour Goods Station; this site was in use from the mid 19th century up until the private siding agreement was terminated on 15 October 1967.

M. Thomas Distribution siding from Lucas Terrace Halt with 20904 passing hauling a weed killing train. 8 April 1990.
BERNARD MILLS

North Quay Junction and a line of wagons for the Gas Works behind a shunters truck. 28 Jun 1962. BLUEBELL RAILWAY MUSEUM J.J. SMITH

Rail cranes

- Fox Elliot & Co. Timber Merchants operated a steam standard gauge rail crane at their Millbay Docks location. It was a Thomas Smith 4wVB lifting 4 tons and supplied new in 1887.
- Shipbreaking Co. Ltd operated adjacent to the Passage House Inn on the Cattewater and acquired from the Admiralty at Devonport a Grafton 4wVB 7 ton standard gauge crane works number 1646 of 1915.

Sources

Hamilton Jenkin, A. K. *Mines of Devon* Landmark Publishing 2005
IRS *Rail Cranes of Devon* (draft)

BR(WR) Monorail use

A monorail system was utilised by British Railways on two sites in the area.

- In 1957 adjacent to North Road Station on the down side, west of the Sutherland Road overbridge, a cutting face was to be cut back adjacent to the live railway. To avoid disruption, a monorail was erected along a narrow ledge, to carry the excavated spoil to above a standard gauge siding,

Monorail west of Sutherland Road bridge. RAILWAY GAZETTE

Mono-rail wagons being loaded with shillet near Plymouth North Road.
RAILWAY GAZETTE,

where it was dumped into open wagons. A 3 h.p. power wagon hauled three tipping skips carrying the spoil. Later the same system was utilised to convey concrete from a mixer to construct the new retaining wall.

- Mono-rail equipment was used in 1956 in connection with the filling up of a disused cutting near Plymouth Friary station, which formerly was the L&SWR Sutton Harbour line.

Source
The Railway Gazette 4 April 1958

Friary Yard Sutton Harbour line cutting infil. 17 October 1956.
MAURICE DART COLLECTION